Fourth Grade Math

with Confidence

Student Workbook

Part B

Fourth Grade Math
with Confidence
Student Workbook
Part B

KATE SNOW

WELL-TRAINED MIND PRESS

Names: Snow, Kate (Teacher), author.

Title: Fourth grade math with confidence. Student workbook part B / Kate Snow.

Other titles: Student workbook part B

Description: [Charles City, Virginia] : Well-Trained Mind Press, [2024] | Series: Math with confidence | Interest age level: 009-010.

Identifiers: ISBN: 978-1-944481-53-7 (paperback)

Subjects: LCSH: Mathematics--Study and teaching (Elementary) | LCGFT: Problems and exercises. | BISAC: JUVENILE NONFICTION / MATHEMATICS / Arithmetic.

Classification: LCC: QA107.2 .S664 2024 | DDC: 372.7--dc23

Reprinted March 2025 by Versa Press, Inc. #J25-01884

Table of Contents

Author's Note

You'll need three books to teach *Fourth Grade Math with Confidence*. All three books are essential for the program.

- The Instructor Guide contains the scripted lesson plans for the entire year (Units 1-16).
- Student Workbook Part A contains the workbook pages for the first half of the year (Units 1-8).
- Student Workbook Part B contains the workbook pages for the second half of the year (Units 9-16).

  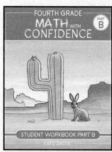

The Student Workbooks are not meant to be used as stand-alone workbooks. The hands-on teaching activities in the Instructor Guide are an essential part of the program. You'll need the directions in the Instructor Guide to guide your child through the Lesson Activities pages. The icon with two heads means that your child should complete these pages with you, and that she is not expected to complete these pages on her own.

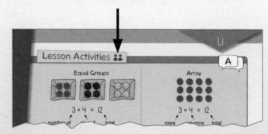

The Practice and Review pages give your child practice with new concepts and review previously-learned skills. The icon with one head means that your child may complete these pages on his own. Most fourth-graders will be able to complete these workbook pages independently, but some may need help reading and interpreting the directions.

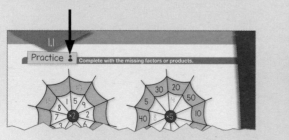 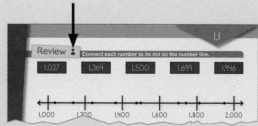

Lesson Activities 👥

Cora

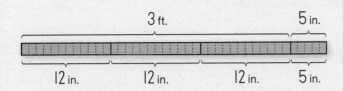

3 ft. 5 in. = ☐ in.

3 × 12 + 5 = ☐

Liam

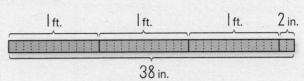

38 in. = ☐ ft. ☐ in.

38 ÷ 12 = ☐

2 ft. = ☐ in.

2 ft. 10 in. = ☐ in.

36 in. = ☐ ft.

37 in. = ☐ ft. ☐ in.

Length Three in a Row

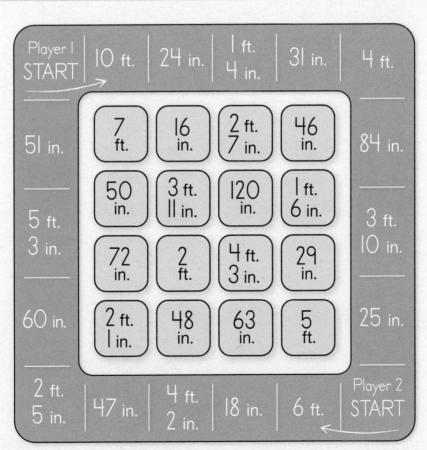

Practice 👤 Complete the chart.

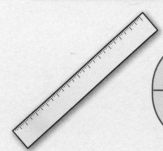

Feet	1	2	3	4	5	6	7	8
Inches	12							

Complete with <, >, or =.

18 in. ◯ 1 ft.   48 in. ◯ 4 ft.   65 in. ◯ 6 ft.

100 in. ◯ 10 ft.   37 in. ◯ 3 ft.   84 in. ◯ 7 ft.

Complete.

1 ft. 10 in. = ☐ in.   27 in. = ☐ ft. ☐ in.

5 ft. 8 in. = ☐ in.   50 in. = ☐ ft. ☐ in.

8 ft. 1 in. = ☐ in.   71 in. = ☐ ft. ☐ in.

Solve.

Emma is 4 feet 6 inches tall.
Rory is 57 inches tall.

- Who is taller?

- How much taller?

The rattlesnake is 40 in. long.
What is its length in feet and inches?

Review 👤 **Convert the mixed numbers to fractions.**

$2\frac{1}{3}$ = ☐

$1\frac{5}{6}$ = ☐

$5\frac{1}{10}$ = ☐

$3\frac{3}{4}$ = ☐

$4\frac{1}{2}$ = ☐

$2\frac{3}{8}$ = ☐

Complete.

4	2	,	9	6	1
+ 8	5	,	4	2	7

1	2	0	,	6	4	5
−	9	3	,	2	4	1

Complete.

$36 \div 12$ = ☐

$72 \div 12$ = ☐

$37 \div 12$ = ☐

$75 \div 12$ = ☐

$48 \div 12$ = ☐

$96 \div 12$ = ☐

$50 \div 12$ = ☐

$100 \div 12$ = ☐

Answer the number riddles.

This number is less than 20.
It has both 2 and 9 as factors.
What is the number?

This number is less than 15. It is prime.
Some of its multiples are 33 and 77.
What is the number?

This number is between 22 and 28.
It is divisible by 5.
What is the number?

 This number is greater than 30 and
less than 60. It is a multiple of 9.
It is not divisible by 6.
What is the number?

Lesson Activities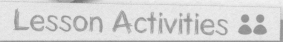

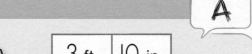

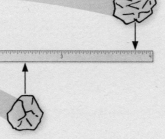

	3 ft.	10 in.
+	2 ft.	7 in.
↺		

	2 ft.	9 in.
+	5 ft.	4 in.
↺		

	3 ft.	8 in.
+	3 ft.	4 in.
↺		

	6 ft.	5 in.
+	7 ft.	2 in.
↺		

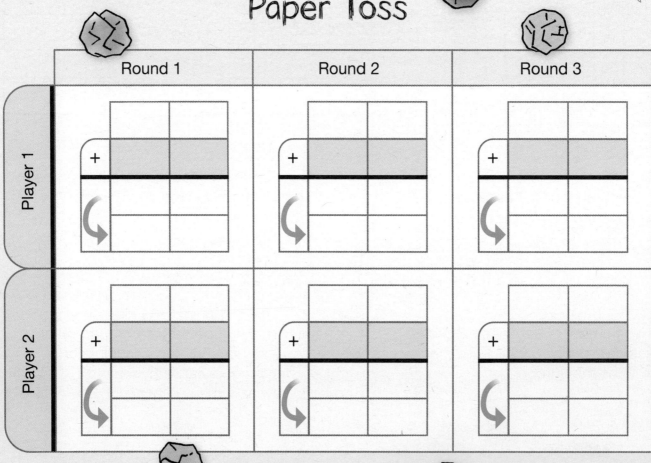

Paper Toss

Practice 👤   Match the equal lengths.

| 18 in. | 13 in. | 15 in. | 23 in. | 20 in. |

| 1 ft. 1 in. | 1 ft. 3 in. | 1 ft. 6 in. | 1 ft. 8 in. | 1 ft. 11 in. |

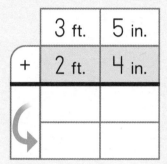

Complete.

	3 ft.	5 in.
+	2 ft.	4 in.

	4 ft.	11 in.
+	1 ft.	5 in.

	4 ft.	9 in.
+	4 ft.	3 in.

	5 ft.	
+	1 ft.	8 in.

	3 ft.	6 in.
+	3 ft.	7 in.

	2 ft.	5 in.
+	6 ft.	7 in.

Solve. Write the equations you use.

Rowan uses two boards to build a birdhouse. One board is 3 feet 4 inches long. The other board is 1 foot 10 inches long. What is the total length of both boards?

Elly uses 2 feet 6 inches of blue tape and 2 feet 6 inches of red tape to make a craft project.
How much tape does she use in all?

9.2

Review 👤 Complete.

	4	5	1
×			7

	6	9	0
×			5

	7	0	8
×			8

Find the area of each shape.

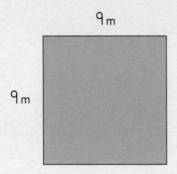

9 m
9 m

Area: _____

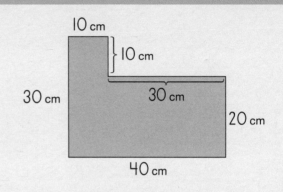

10 cm
10 cm
30 cm
30 cm
20 cm
40 cm

Area: _____

Convert the fractions to mixed numbers or whole numbers.

$\frac{17}{5}$ = ____

$\frac{24}{3}$ = ____

$\frac{11}{2}$ = ____

$\frac{29}{10}$ = ____

$\frac{21}{4}$ = ____

$\frac{18}{6}$ = ____

Use the clues to complete the chart.

- Aria scored 40 points.

- Clare scored 3 times as many points as Aria.

- Clare scored 2 times as many points as Everett.

Name	Points
Aria	
Clare	
Everett	

Lesson Activities 👥

A

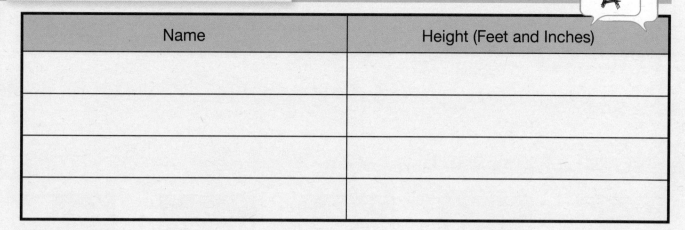

Name	Height (Feet and Inches)

B

You have 3 feet 2 inches of ribbon.
If you use 1 foot 8 inches,
how much ribbon will you have left?

	3 ft.	2 in.
−	1 ft.	8 in.

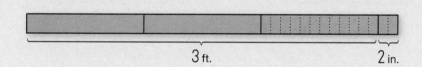

3 ft.   2 in.

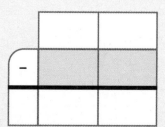

	6 ft.	1 in.
−	3 ft.	8 in.

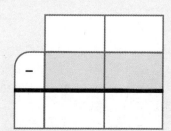

	4 ft.	
−	1 ft.	3 in.

	5 ft.	5 in.
−	1 ft.	9 in.

C

Practice 👤 Match the equal lengths.

| 5 ft. | 3 ft. 2 in. | 4 ft. 6 in. | 3 ft. 5 in. | 4 ft. 1 in. |

| 2 ft. 14 in. | 4 ft. 12 in. | 3 ft. 18 in. | 3 ft. 13 in. | 2 ft. 17 in. |

Complete.

	5 ft.	6 in.
−	3 ft.	2 in.

	7 ft.	1 in.
−	4 ft.	7 in.

	6 ft.	
−	2 ft.	8 in.

	8 ft.	3 in.
−	5 ft.	6 in.

	10 ft.	
−	8 ft.	4 in.

	4 ft.	9 in.
−	2 ft.	5 in.

Solve. Write the equations you use.

At the petting zoo, the horse is
8 feet 2 inches long. The donkey is
5 feet 7 inches long. How much longer
is the horse than the donkey?

The goat is 2 feet 10 inches long.
The sheep is 4 feet 1 inch long.
How much longer is the sheep
than the goat?

Review Complete.

	5	$\frac{5}{6}$
+	2	

	6	
+	4	$\frac{2}{3}$

	5	$\frac{5}{6}$
–	2	

	6	
–	4	$\frac{2}{3}$

Write whether each angle is acute, right, obtuse, or straight.

[_____]

[_____]

[_____]

[_____]

[_____]

[_____]

Complete.

$20 \div 5 =$ [_____]

$72 \div 12 =$ [_____]

$56 \div 8 =$ [_____]

$36 \div$ [_____] $= 6$

$40 \div$ [_____] $= 5$

$84 \div$ [_____] $= 7$

[_____] $\div 7 = 3$

[_____] $\div 11 = 9$

$54 \div 9 =$ [_____]

$64 \div 8 =$ [_____]

[_____] $\div 6 = 7$

[_____] $\div 12 = 8$

Lesson Activities 👥

Sam

8 yd.

3 ft.

8 yd. = ☐ ft.

8 × 3 = ☐

Liza

1 yd.

21 ft.

21 ft. = ☐ yd.

21 ÷ 3 = ☐

Yards

4 yd.

10 yd.

30 yd.

3 yd.

☐ yd.

☐ yd.

☐ yd.

☐ yd.

Feet

☐ ft.

☐ ft.

☐ ft.

☐ ft.

60 ft.

15 ft.

18 ft.

27 ft.

Stillwater Pond

Forest Falls

1 mile

2 miles

Parking

1 mile

3 miles

Lookout Rock

1 mile = 5,280 ft.

Distance (Miles)	Distance (Feet)

Practice

Complete the chart.

Yards	1	2	3	4	5	6	7	8
Feet								

Complete.

9 yd. = ☐ ft.

10 yd. = ☐ ft.

30 yd. = ☐ ft.

40 yd. = ☐ ft.

100 yd. = ☐ ft.

30 ft. = ☐ yd.

33 ft. = ☐ yd.

36 ft. = ☐ yd.

60 ft. = ☐ yd.

150 ft. = ☐ yd.

Solve.

Brielle bikes 6 miles.
Each mile is 5,280 feet.
How many feet does she bike?

Nathanael runs 500 yards.
How many feet does he run?

The swimming pool is 25 yards long.
How many feet long is it?

Calvin needs 3 yards of ribbon for a craft project. How many inches of ribbon does he need?

Review 👤 Choose the more reasonable measurement for each angle.

| 80° | 100° | | 80° | 100° | | 90° | 120° |

Complete. Follow the steps.

| 1. Divide |
| 2. Multiply |
| 3. Subtract |

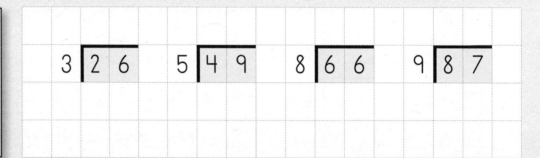

$$3\overline{)2\ 6} \qquad 5\overline{)4\ 9} \qquad 8\overline{)6\ 6} \qquad 9\overline{)8\ 7}$$

Use a ruler to draw a line with the given length.

$3\dfrac{1}{2}$ in.

$2\dfrac{1}{4}$ in.

$3\dfrac{3}{4}$ in.

Lesson Activities 👥

	7 ft.	8 in.
+	3 ft.	5 in.

	9 ft.	4 in.
-	5 ft.	9 in.

CRAFT STORE HELP DESK

I have 4 yards of striped ribbon and 8 feet of solid-colored ribbon. How many feet of ribbon do I have in all?

I'm knitting a scarf. So far, I've knit 18 inches. I want the scarf to be 5 feet long. How many more inches do I need to knit?

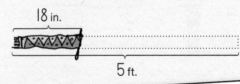

18 in.

5 ft.

I want to make a square picture frame with 16 in. sides. I need to know how much wood to buy. What's the frame's perimeter in feet and inches?

I have 3 feet of string. If I cut the string into 4 equal pieces, how many inches long will each piece be?

16 in.

3 ft.

Practice 👤 Complete.

	4 ft.	11 in.
+	2 ft.	9 in.
↺		

	6 ft.	3 in.
-	4 ft.	1 in.

	5 ft.	4 in.
-	4 ft.	8 in.

Solve. Write the equations you use.

Aubrey sews together two pieces of fabric to make a flag.
One piece of fabric is 18 inches long.
The other piece is 2 feet long.
What is the total length of the flag in inches?

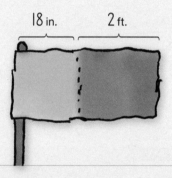

18 in.   2 ft.

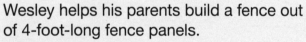

Cameron helps his mom saw a 6-foot log into two parts.
One part is 30 inches long.
How many inches long is the other part?

6 ft.

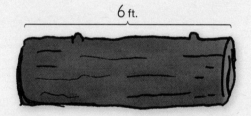

Wesley helps his parents build a fence out of 4-foot-long fence panels.
They use 6 panels.
How many yards long is the fence?

4 ft.

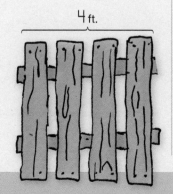

Freya has a 5-foot long board.
She cuts it into 6-inch-long pieces.
How many pieces does she get?

5 ft.

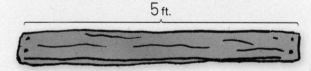

Review Use a protractor to measure the angles.

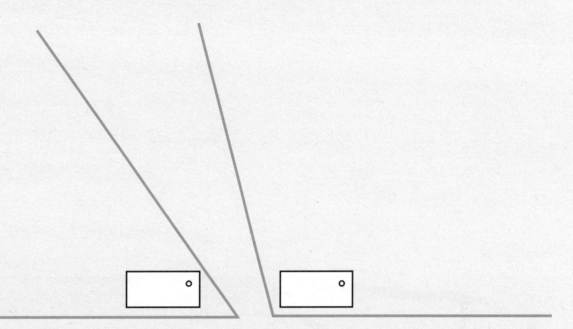

Complete.

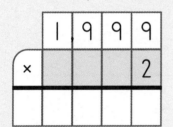 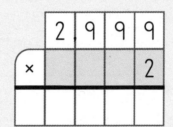 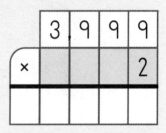

Round each number to the underlined place.	Complete.
4,8<u>2</u>3 ≈	240 ÷ 4 =
6,4<u>8</u>1 ≈	300 ÷ 6 =
3,<u>9</u>75 ≈	2,400 ÷ 4 =
<u>8</u>4,623 ≈	3,000 ÷ 6 =

Lesson Activities 👥

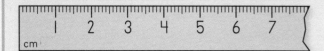

1 centimeter = 10 millimeters

4 cm 3 mm = ☐ mm

4 × 10 + 3 = ☐

37 mm = ☐ cm ☐ mm

37 ÷ 10 = ☐

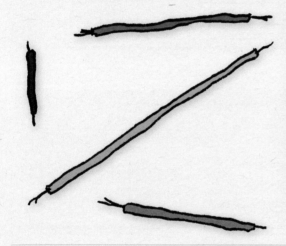

Wire	Length (cm and mm)	Length (mm)
Red		
Green		
Blue		
Black		

Measurement Tag

PLAYER
2
START

PLAYER
1
START

Practice 👤

**Draw a line that matches each measurement.
Then, complete the conversion.**

4 cm 8 mm = [ ] mm

32 mm = [ ] cm [ ] mm

1 cm 6 mm = [ ] mm

29 mm = [ ] cm [ ] mm

6 cm 5 mm = [ ] mm

53 mm = [ ] cm [ ] mm

Complete with <, >, or =.

4 mm ◯ 4 cm

67 mm ◯ 8 cm

54 mm ◯ 3 cm

42 mm ◯ 4 cm

50 mm ◯ 5 cm

79 mm ◯ 8 cm

Solve.

The grasshopper's body is 32 mm long. What is its length in centimeters and millimeters?

The monarch butterfly has a wingspan of 9 cm 2 mm.
What is its wingspan in millimeters?

Review 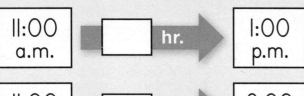 Complete.

	9	9
×		5

	9	9
×		6

	9	9
×		7

	9	9
×		8

	9	9
×		9

Complete.

11:00 a.m. → ☐ hr. → 1:00 p.m.

11:00 a.m. → ☐ hr. → 3:00 p.m.

9:00 a.m. → ☐ hr. → 2:00 p.m.

9:00 a.m. → ☐ hr. → 4:00 p.m.

8:00 a.m. → ☐ hr. → 5:00 p.m.

Complete.

$700 \div 100 =$ ☐

$400 \div 100 =$ ☐

$1,000 \div 100 =$ ☐

$2,000 \div 1,000 =$ ☐

$5,000 \div 1,000 =$ ☐

$9,000 \div 1,000 =$ ☐

Solve. Write the equations you use.

Edith has 16 feet of rope. She cuts the rope into as many 3-foot pieces as she can. How many feet of rope does she have left over?

Elliot throws the frisbee $9\frac{6}{10}$ m. Ahren throws the frisbee $2\frac{3}{10}$ m farther than Elliot. How far does Ahren throw the frisbee?

Lesson Activities

 1 meter = 100 centimeters

Women's Olympic
High Jump Record:
2 m 6 cm

2 m 6 cm = [ ] cm

2 × 100 + 6 = [ ]

Men's Olympic
High Jump Record:
239 cm

239 cm = [ ] m [ ] cm

239 ÷ 100 = [ ]

B

Women's Olympic Records

Event	Pole Vault 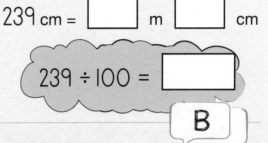	Long Jump	Triple Jump
Record (m and cm)	5 m 5 cm	7 m 40 cm	15 m 67 cm
Record (cm)			

Men's Olympic Records

Event	Pole Vault	Long Jump	Triple Jump
Record (m and cm)			
Record (cm)	603 cm	890 cm	1,809 cm

Practice

Complete the chart.

Meters	1	2	3	4	5	6
Centimeters						

Complete with <, >, or =.

99 cm ◯ 1 m   246 cm ◯ 2 m   300 cm ◯ 3 m

6 m ◯ 438 cm   10 m ◯ 1,500 cm   20 m ◯ 2,000 cm

Complete.

2 m 50 cm = ☐ cm   672 cm = ☐ m ☐ cm

4 m 7 cm = ☐ cm   901 cm = ☐ m ☐ cm

Solve.

The red paper airplane flew 5 meters 30 centimeters. The yellow paper airplane flew 490 centimeters.

- Which airplane flew farther?

- How much farther?

Oliver threw the football 9 meters 75 centimeters.
Cannon threw the football 990 centimeters.

- Who threw the football farther?

- How much farther?

Review 👤 Find the missing angle measures.

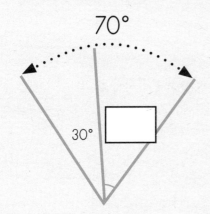

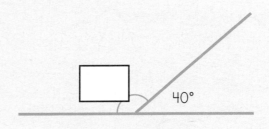

Circle the fractions that match the description.
X the fractions that do not match the description.

Less than 1 whole	Equal to 1 whole	Greater than 1 whole

$$\frac{7}{10} \qquad \frac{4}{3} \qquad \frac{5}{8} \qquad \frac{4}{4} \qquad \frac{12}{6} \qquad \frac{10}{10} \qquad \frac{2}{3} \qquad \frac{12}{10} \qquad \frac{5}{5}$$

$$\frac{9}{8} \qquad \frac{3}{2} \qquad \frac{3}{4} \qquad \frac{6}{7} \qquad \frac{7}{8} \qquad \frac{15}{3} \qquad \frac{3}{2} \qquad \frac{4}{5} \qquad \frac{30}{10}$$

Match.

$64 \div 8$	$42 \div 7$	$56 \div 8$	$54 \div 6$

6	7	8	9

$56 \div 7$	$48 \div 8$	$63 \div 7$	$49 \div 7$

9.8

Lesson Activities 👥

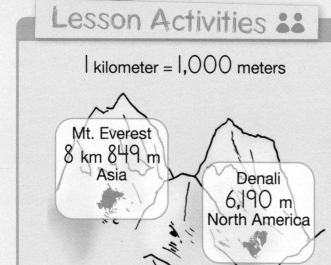

A

1 kilometer = 1,000 meters

Mt. Everest
8 km 849 m
Asia

Denali
6,190 m
North America

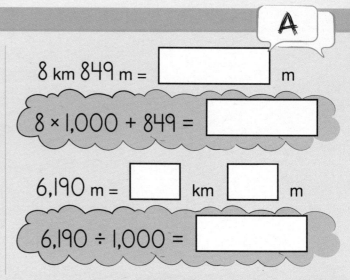

8 km 849 m = ⬜ m

8 × 1,000 + 849 = ⬜

6,190 m = ⬜ km ⬜ m

6,190 ÷ 1,000 = ⬜

	Continent	Mountain	Elevation (km and m)	Elevation (m)
	South America	Aconcagua	6 km 961 m	
	Africa	Kilimanjaro	5 km 895 m	
	Antarctica	Mount Vinson		4,892 m
	Europe	Mont Blanc		4,810 m
	Australia	Mount Kosciuszko		2,228 m

B

Why did the obtuse angle lose the argument?

(V) 7 cm → mm

(T) 7 m → cm

(G) 7 m 20 cm → cm

(N) 70 cm → mm

(H) 700 cm → m

(R) 72 cm → mm

(I) 7,000 m → km

(E) 72,000 m → km

Because it's...

700
mm
72
km
70
mm
72
km
720
mm

720
mm
7
km
720
cm
7
m
700
cm

Practice 👤   Complete with <, >, or =.

4,070 m ◯ 4 km   6,000 m ◯ 6 km   1,999 m ◯ 2 km

3,600 m ◯ 3 km   9,587 m ◯ 12 km   8,000 m ◯ 8 km

Complete.

4 km = [ ] m   5,000 m = [ ] km

4 km 128 m = [ ] m   5,315 m = [ ] km [ ] m

7 km = [ ] m   10,000 m = [ ] km

7 km 9 m = [ ] m   10,030 m = [ ] km [ ] m

Asher made a chart of how many laps he ran each day. Complete the chart to show how far he ran each day.

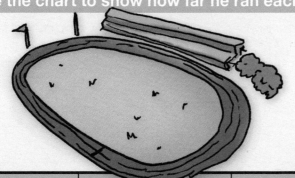

Each lap is **400** meters long

Day	Number of Laps	Distance (m)	Distance (km and m)
Monday	3	1,200 m	
Tuesday	6		
Wednesday	5		
Thursday	8		
Friday	10		

Review

Use a protractor to draw an angle with the given measure. Use the printed line for one side. Use the dot for the vertex.

35°

125°

Write tens, hundreds, or thousands to complete the blanks.

100 = 10 | tens |

200 = 20 | |

230 = 23 | |

400 = 4 | |

400 = 40 | |

1,000 = 10 | hundreds |

2,500 = 25 | |

3,000 = 3 | |

3,000 = 30 | |

★ 3,000 = 300 | |

Solve. Write the equations you use.

Zaidee's neighbor pays her $5 for walking his dog. He pays her $10 for mowing his lawn. If she walks the dog 6 times and mows the lawn 4 times, how much will she earn?

Nolan has $8.75.
He buys candy for $4.39.
How much money does he have left?

Lesson 9.8

Lesson Activities

A

1 cm = [ ] mm

1 m = [ ] cm

1 km = [ ] m

6 cm 13 mm = 7 cm [ ] mm

7 m 140 cm = 8 m [ ] cm

4 cm 5 mm = 3 cm [ ] mm

2 m 30 cm = 1 m [ ] cm

The red wire is 7 cm 4 mm long. The blue wire is 2 cm 8 mm long.

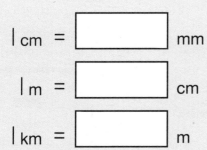

What is the total length of both wires?

7 cm	4 mm
+ 2 cm	8 mm

How much longer is the red wire than the blue wire?

7 cm	4 mm
− 2 cm	8 mm

Damien has two pipes. One pipe is 4 m 25 cm. The other pipe is 2 m 80 cm.

What is the total length of both pipes?

4 m	25 cm
+ 2 m	80 cm

What is the difference between the lengths of the pipes?

4 m	25 cm
− 2 m	80 cm

Betty ran 6 km on Monday. She ran 4 km 200 m on Tuesday.

How far did she run in all?

6 km	
+ 4 km	200 m

How much farther did she run on Monday than Tuesday?

6 km	
− 4 km	200 m

Practice 👤 | Complete.

	5 cm	6 mm
+	2 cm	4 mm
↻		

	3 m	60 cm
+	4 m	90 cm
↻		

	2 km	500 m
+	3 km	600 m
↻		

	7 cm	2 mm
−	4 cm	7 mm

	6 m	90 cm
−	2 m	30 cm

	4 km	100 m
−	2 km	400 m

Solve. Write the equations you use.

Reuben has 18 cm 5 mm of wire for a robotics project. He uses 12 cm 8 mm. How much wire does he have left?

The North Trail is 3 km 400 m.
The East Trail is 2 km 900 m.
If Eleanor's family hikes both trails, how far will they hike?

Hailey builds a fence with two panels.
One panel is 4 m 75 cm long.
The other panel is 6 m 25 cm long.
What is the total length of the fence?

Dylan has 4 m of yarn.
He uses 2 m 40 cm for a craft.
How much yarn does he have left?

Review Complete the chart.

Standard Form	Expanded Form
28,035	
150,960	
	70,000 + 400 + 8
	900,000 + 60,000 + 30 + 2

Complete each blank with the greatest number possible.

10 × [7] < 73   5 × [ ] < 26

6 × [ ] < 40   7 × [ ] < 24

8 × [ ] < 35   9 × [ ] < 37

4 × [ ] < 30   3 × [ ] < 31

Find all possible factor pairs for each number.

Factor pairs of 40

Factor pairs of 23

Complete. Follow the steps.

1. Divide
2. Multiply
3. Subtract

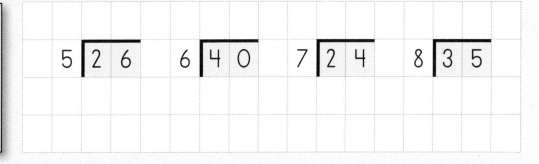

$5\overline{)26}$ $6\overline{)40}$ $7\overline{)24}$ $8\overline{)35}$

Lesson Activities

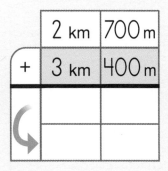

	2 km	700 m
+	3 km	400 m

	12 m	30 cm
-	5 m	90 cm

	8 cm	3 mm
-	5 cm	1 mm

On Monday, Mateo runs 3 km.
On Tuesday, he runs 750 m.
How many meters does he run in all?

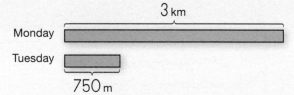

Monday — 3 km
Tuesday — 750 m

Hazel wants to run 2 km.
So far, she has run 800 m.
How many more meters does she need to run to accomplish her goal?

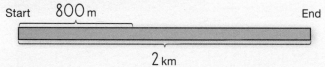

Start — 800 m — End
2 km

Gianna tapes together 6 pieces of paper to make a banner.
Each piece of paper is 30 cm long.
What is the total length of the banner in meters and centimeters?

HAPPY BIRTHDAY!
30 cm

Muhammad uses wire to make jewelry.
He has a piece of wire 3 cm long.
He cuts the wire into 2 equal pieces.
How long is each piece in millimeters?

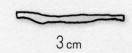

3 cm

Practice Complete.

	7 cm	5 mm
+	6 cm	5 mm

	8 m	20 cm
−	5 m	80 cm

	4 km	
−	1 km	600 m

Solve. Write the equations you use.

Xavier has 6 boards.
Each board is 75 cm long.
What is the total length of the boards in meters and centimeters?

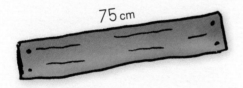
75 cm

Amara uses 9 cm of red wire and 54 mm of yellow wire for an electrical repair.
How many millimeters of wire does she use in all?

Sadie has 4 meters of string.
She cuts the string into 5 equal pieces.
How long is each piece in centimeters?

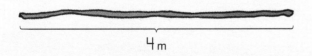
4 m

Jordan has 3 m of rope.
He uses 85 cm in his tree fort.
How many centimeters of rope does he have left?

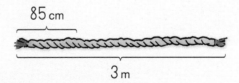
85 cm
3 m

Review   Match.

| 56 ÷ 7 | | 7 | | 64 ÷ 8 |

| 57 ÷ 7 | | 7 RI | | 65 ÷ 8 |

| 49 ÷ 7 | | 8 | | 56 ÷ 8 |

| 50 ÷ 7 | | 8 RI | | 57 ÷ 8 |

Use a ruler to draw a line with the given length.

9 cm 5 mm

95 mm

$3\frac{3}{4}$ in.

Complete.

	1	,	8	9	0
×					7

	3	,	6	0	2
×					8

	8	,	9	4	1
×					9

Unit Wrap-Up 👤

Complete with <, >, or =.

12 in. = 1 ft.	
3 ft. = 1 yd.	
5,280 ft. = 1 mi.	

35 in. ◯ 3 ft.   62 in. ◯ 5 ft.

12 ft. ◯ 4 yd.   60 ft. ◯ 30 yd.

1 mi. ◯ 5,000 ft.   2 mi. ◯ 10,000 ft.

Complete.

	4 ft.	5 in.
+	3 ft.	10 in.
↺		

	3 ft.	2 in.
−	1 ft.	8 in.

	9 ft.	
−	3 ft.	7 in.

Solve. Write the equations you use.

The orca whale is 24 feet long.
What is its length in yards?

Valentina walks 4 miles.
How many feet does she walk?

Noah is 3 feet 11 inches tall.
His friend Stevie is 50 inches tall.
How much taller is Stevie than Noah?

Iris has 2 feet 8 inches of yarn.
She cuts the yarn into 4 equal pieces.
How many inches long is each piece?

Unit Wrap-Up 👤 Complete.

| 1 cm = 10 mm | 1 m = 100 cm | 1 km = 1,000 m |

8 cm = [ ] mm

4 m = [ ] cm

6 km = [ ] m

90 mm = [ ] cm

700 cm = [ ] m

9,000 m = [ ] km

40 mm = [ ] cm

1,000 cm = [ ] m

7,000 m = [ ] km

Complete.

	10 cm	3 mm
+	15 cm	8 mm
↻		

	6 km	100 m
-	3 km	900 m

	8 m	
-	4 m	25 cm

Solve. Write the equations you use.

Michael bikes 12 km.
How many meters does he bike?

Ayla builds a picture frame with six sides.
Each side is 20 cm long.
What is the picture frame's perimeter in meters and centimeters?

20 cm

The worm is 10 cm 2 mm long.
What is its length in millimeters?

Lincoln jumps 84 cm.
Leo jumps 39 cm farther than Lincoln.
How far does Leo jump in meters and centimeters?

Lesson Activities 👥

1. Divide
2. Multiply
3. Subtract

9 ⌐1 2   8 ⌐1 7   6 ⌐2 4   9 ⌐2 0

4 children share 5 candies.

4 ⌐5

5 children share 4 candies.

5 ⌐4

3 ⌐5   5 ⌐3   2 ⌐4   4 ⌐2   8 ⌐1   1 ⌐8

Zero or One?

Start 3 ⌐4   7 ⌐9   6 ⌐5   5 ⌐2   9 ⌐10

9 ⌐7   5 ⌐7   8 ⌐6   7 ⌐7   2 ⌐3   6 ⌐4

4 ⌐6   2 ⌐3   7 ⌐1   3 ⌐2   4 ⌐7   4 ⌐2

Finish 3 ⌐1   6 ⌐8   2 ⌐1   8 ⌐9   5 ⌐5

Practice 👤 **Label the parts of the division problem.**

6 ← [_____]

[_____] → 3 ⟌ 18 ← [_____]

quotient

dividend

divisor

Complete.

1. Divide
2. Multiply
3. Subtract

2 ⟌ 9   5 ⟌ 8   4 ⟌ 7   6 ⟌ 5   7 ⟌ 4

2 ⟌ 1 9   5 ⟌ 3 2   4 ⟌ 2 9   7 ⟌ 3 8   6 ⟌ 2 1

Match.

4 ⟌ 5   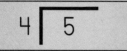 0 R4   6 ⟌ 4

5 ⟌ 4   1 R1   6 ⟌ 7

4 ⟌ 6   1 R2   5 ⟌ 7

Review

Complete.

$(6 \times 5) + 3 = \boxed{}$

$(12 \times 7) + 2 = \boxed{}$

$(8 \times 9) + 3 = \boxed{}$

$(11 \times 7) + 2 = \boxed{}$

$(7 \times 5) + 1 = \boxed{}$

Complete with <, >, or =.

$\dfrac{3}{2} \bigcirc 1$

$\dfrac{7}{8} \bigcirc \dfrac{6}{8}$

$1\dfrac{2}{5} \bigcirc 1\dfrac{4}{5}$

$2\dfrac{2}{3} \bigcirc \dfrac{8}{3}$

Complete.

+	3 ft.	9 in.
2 ft.	5 in.	

-	6 ft.	1 in.
3 ft.	8 in.	

-	10 ft.	5 in.
4 ft.	7 in.	

Solve. Write the equations you use.

Evelyn makes 6 bracelets.
She uses 144 beads for each bracelet.
How many beads does she use in all?

Braden has 4 pieces of rope.
Each piece is 235 cm long.
How many centimeters of rope does he have in all?

Lesson Activities

	4	9	7
+	2	3	1

	6	7	4
−	2	5	8

	1	5	4
×			3

5 | 3 7

Scott has 29 candy hearts.
He splits them into 4 equal groups
to give to his family.
How many are in each group?

4 × 6 = ☐

4 × 8 = ☐

4 × 7 = ☐

4 | 2 9

Don't Go Over!

2 2   2 3   2 6   2 9

3 1   3 3   3 4   3 7

3 8   3 9   4 1   4 3

Player 1	Player 2

Practice
Complete each blank with the greatest possible number.

$3 \times \boxed{3} < 11$ $6 \times \boxed{} < 14$ $5 \times \boxed{} < 19$

$6 \times \boxed{} < 8$ $6 \times \boxed{} < 4$ $5 \times \boxed{} < 12$

$9 \times \boxed{} < 23$ $7 \times \boxed{} < 30$ $8 \times \boxed{} < 41$

Complete. Follow the steps.

1. Divide
2. Multiply
3. Subtract

$6\overline{)7}$ $7\overline{)6}$ $5\overline{)8}$ $8\overline{)5}$ $9\overline{)3}$

$6\overline{)32}$ $7\overline{)48}$ $8\overline{)65}$ $9\overline{)73}$ $4\overline{)37}$

Solve. Write the equations you use.

The ribbon is 28 inches long.
Ava cuts it into 4 equal pieces.
How long is each piece?

Hugo bakes 60 cookies.
He divides them equally into 3 boxes.
How many cookies are in each box?

Review

Circle the numbers that match the description.
X the numbers that do not match the description.

Multiples of 6		
21	35	42
24	36	48

Multiples of 7		
21	35	42
24	36	48

Multiples of 8		
21	35	42
24	36	48

Divisible by 6		
21	35	42
24	36	48

Divisible by 7		
21	35	42
24	36	48

Divisible by 8		
21	35	42
24	36	48

Complete.

31 − 28 = ☐

40 − 36 = ☐

22 − 17 = ☐

51 − 49 = ☐

44 − 36 = ☐

Complete.

	6 km	400 m
+	3 km	600 m

	7 cm	2 mm
−	3 cm	8 mm

	5 m	
−	1 m	70 cm

Solve. Write the equations you use.

Bryant buys 4 shirts. Each shirt costs $18.
He also buys a pair of pants for $25.
How much does he spend in all?

Sanvi has 50 chairs to set up for the
speech contest. She makes 6 rows of
8 chairs and puts the extra chairs away.
How many chairs does she put away?

Lesson Activities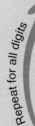

A

1. Divide

2. Multiply

3. Subtract

4. Bring down the next digit (if needed)

Repeat for all digits

Dirty **M**onkeys **S**mell **B**ad

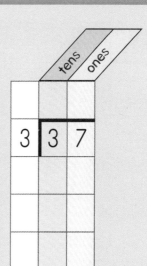

	tens	ones
3	3	7

B

Lemonade Stand Earnings

Day	Dollars
1	$ 37
2	$ 64
3	$ 68
4	$ 95
5	$ 98

	tens	ones
3	6	4

	tens	ones
3	6	8

	tens	ones
3	9	5

	tens	ones
3	9	8

10.3

Practice — Complete.

```
        1. Divide

        2. Multiply

        3. Subtract

        4. Bring down the next digit (if needed)
```

Repeat (if needed)

		tens	ones			tens	ones			tens	ones			tens	ones
	2	4	7		4	4	6		5	5	7		4	8	9

Solve. Use the completed problems above to find the answers.

Ian has 46 pea seeds.
He plants them in 4 equal rows.

- How many seeds are in each row?

- How many seeds are left over?

Blair has 47 flowers to plant.
She plants the flowers in 2 groups and makes the groups as equal as possible. How many are in each group?

Review

Complete the fact family.

$8 \times 7 = \boxed{}$

$\boxed{} \times \boxed{} = \boxed{}$

$\boxed{} \div \boxed{} = \boxed{}$

$\boxed{} \div \boxed{} = \boxed{}$

Complete.

6 ft. = $\boxed{}$ in.

48 in. = $\boxed{}$ ft.

15 ft. = $\boxed{}$ yd.

8 yd. = $\boxed{}$ ft.

Find the missing angle measure.

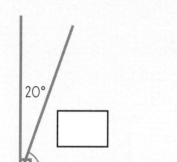

20°

Complete.

$(4 \times 9) + 3 = \boxed{}$

$(6 \times 8) + 1 = \boxed{}$

$(5 \times 20) + 6 = \boxed{}$

$(3 \times 40) + 12 = \boxed{}$

Solve. Write the equations you use.

The campers at summer camp split into 3 teams to play a group game. There are 38 children on each team. How many children are there in all?

Some of the campers hike 5 miles. How many feet do they hike? (Each mile is 5,280 feet.)

Lesson Activities 👥

1. Divide

2. Multiply

3. Subtract

4. Bring down the next digit (if needed)

Repeat (if needed)

	tens	ones			tens	ones			tens	ones	
3	6	5		2	5	3		5	7	5	

Roll and Divide

Player 1

| 8 | 3 | | 9 | 6 | | 7 | 7 | | 7 | 2 |

Sum of remainders

Player 2

| 8 | 3 | | 9 | 6 | | 7 | 7 | | 7 | 2 |

Sum of remainders

Practice

Complete. Follow the steps.

1. Divide

2. Multiply

3. Subtract

4. Bring down the next digit (if needed)

Repeat (if needed)

	tens	ones		tens	ones		tens	ones		tens	ones		tens	ones
2	8	9	5	8	5	4	7	0	3	5	1	2	6	8

Solve. Use the completed problems above to answer the questions.

Carol spends $68 to buy 2 lamps.
Each lamp costs the same amount.
How much does each lamp cost?

5 friends work together to earn $85.
They split the money equally.
How much money does each friend earn?

Review 👤 Match.

one hundred thousand one	101,000
one hundred one thousand	110,000
one hundred thousand ten	100,001
one hundred ten thousand	100,100
one hundred thousand one hundred	100,010

Complete.

12:00 p.m. → [ ] min. → 12:45 p.m.

12:00 p.m. → [ ] hr. → 2:00 p.m.

12:00 p.m. → [ ] hr. [ ] min. → 2:30 p.m.

12:00 p.m. → [ ] hr. [ ] min. → 6:15 p.m.

Complete.

$13 + 7 = 15 + \boxed{}$

$\boxed{} + 8 = 4 + 9$

$35 - 7 = 30 - \boxed{}$

$50 - \boxed{} = 42 + 4$

Choose the more sensible unit for each item.

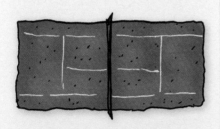
Area of a tennis court

250 sq. m	250 sq. km

Area of a sandbox

24 sq. in.	24 sq. ft.

Area of a welcome mat

600 sq. in.	600 sq. ft.

Lesson Activities 👥

1. Divide
2. Multiply
3. Subtract
4. Bring down the next digit (if needed)

Repeat (if needed)

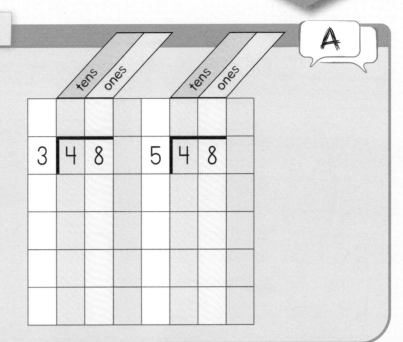

tens	ones			tens	ones
3	4	8		5	4	8

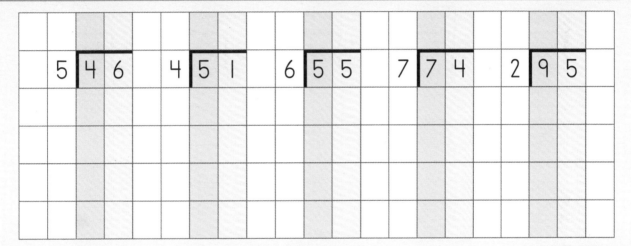

| | 5 | 4 | 6 | | 4 | 5 | 1 | | 6 | 5 | 5 | | 7 | 7 | 4 | | 2 | 9 | 5 |

How Many Digits?

Start | 3 ⟌ 26 | 7 ⟌ 59 | 6 ⟌ 93 | 5 ⟌ 32 | 9 ⟌ 93

9 ⟌ 78 | 5 ⟌ 67 | 8 ⟌ 61 | 7 ⟌ 67 | 2 ⟌ 34 | 6 ⟌ 50

4 ⟌ 49 | 2 ⟌ 17 | 7 ⟌ 85 | 3 ⟌ 25 | 4 ⟌ 65 | 4 ⟌ 30

Finish | 3 ⟌ 56 | 6 ⟌ 79 | 2 ⟌ 19 | 8 ⟌ 84 | 5 ⟌ 46

Practice  **Complete. Follow the steps.**

1. Divide

2. Multiply

3. Subtract

4. Bring down the next digit (if needed)

Repeat (if needed)

7 | 8 6   5 | 3 3   4 | 6 5

4 | 8 4   9 | 7 5   7 | 7 9   6 | 8 0   5 | 3 6

Solve. Use the completed problems above to answer the questions.

Mallory has 36 chairs to arrange for the performance.
She makes 5 equal rows of chairs.

- How many chairs are in each row?

- How many extra chairs does she have?

Annabelle buys 4 shirts. She spends $84.
Each shirt costs the same amount.
What is the price of each shirt?

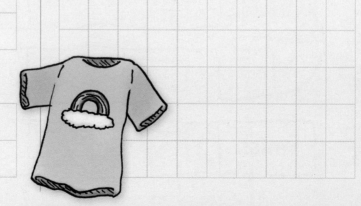

Review

Complete the chart.

Standard Form	Expanded Form
26,074	
305,009	
	200,000 + 70,000 + 400
	50,000 + 600 + 80 + 3

Complete.

60 mm = [   ] cm

8 cm = [   ] mm

300 cm = [   ] m

9 m = [   ] cm

4,000 m = [   ] km

5 km = [   ] m

Complete.

4,000 × [   ] = 8,000

3,000 × [   ] = 15,000

2,000 × [   ] = 14,000

9,000 ÷ [   ] = 3,000

7,000 ÷ [   ] = 1,000

10,000 ÷ [   ] = 2,000

Choose the more sensible unit for each item.

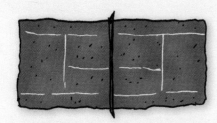

Perimeter of a tennis court

70 cm	70 m

Perimeter of a sandbox

20 in.	20 ft.

Perimeter of a welcome mat

100 in.	100 ft.

Lesson Activities 👥

A

	hundreds	tens	ones			hundreds	tens	ones
2	2	3	5		3	2	3	5

Repeat (if needed)

1. Divide

2. Multiply

3. Subtract

4. Bring down the next digit (if needed)

B

The Quotient Game

Player 1	Player 2

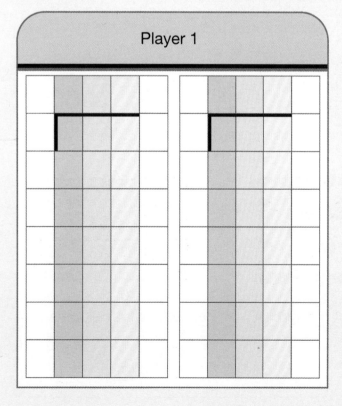

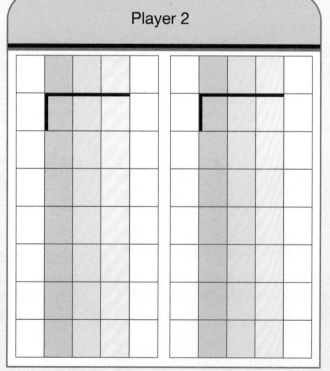

Practice

Complete. Follow the steps.

1. Divide

2. Multiply

3. Subtract

4. Bring down the next digit (if needed)

Repeat (if needed)

| 5 ⟌ 9 3 2 | 2 ⟌ 8 1 5 | 4 ⟌ 2 1 9 | 3 ⟌ 1 5 9 |

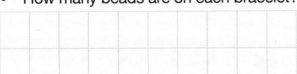

Solve. Use the completed problems above to help find the answers.

Owen has 219 beads.
He makes 4 bracelets and puts the same number of beads on each bracelet.

• How many beads are on each bracelet?

• How many extra beads does he have?

Isabella has 159 centimeters of ribbon.
She cuts the ribbon into 3 equal pieces.
How long is each piece?

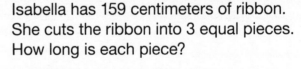

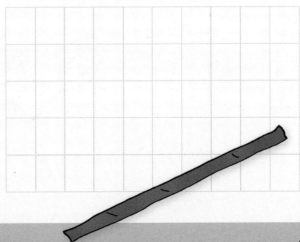

Lesson 10.6

49

Review

Complete.

5 cm = [ ] mm

5 cm 2 mm = [ ] mm

12 m = [ ] cm

12 m 80 cm = [ ] cm

8,000 m = [ ] km

8,195 m = [ ] km [ ] m

500 cm = [ ] m

538 cm = [ ] m [ ] cm

Use the chart to complete the bar graph. Then, answer the questions.

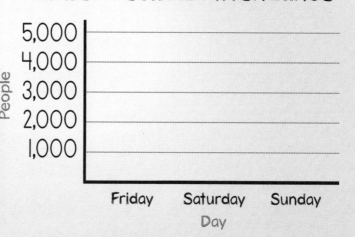

Day	Number of People
Friday	2,467
Saturday	4,391
Sunday	3,832

Winter Festival Attendance

How many more people attended on Saturday than on Friday?

How many people attended in all?

Lesson Activities 👥

1. Divide

2. Multiply

3. Subtract

4. Bring down the next digit (if needed)

Repeat (if needed)

| 2 | 7 | 6 | 4 | | 4 | 4 | 1 | 9 | | 3 | 2 | 1 | 2 |

B

Two friends work together to earn $764.
They split the money equally.
How much does each friend earn?

Check:

A baker makes 419 cookies. She arranges the cookies on 4 trays and puts the same number of cookies on each tray.

- How many cookies are on each tray?

Check:

- How many cookies are left over?

A baker makes 212 muffins.
He puts 3 muffins in each box.

- How many boxes does he fill?

Check:

- How many muffins are left over?

10.7

Practice

**Complete. Follow the steps.
Then, multiply (or multiply and add) to check your answers.**

1. Divide

2. Multiply

3. Subtract

4. Bring down the next digit (if needed)

Repeat (if needed)

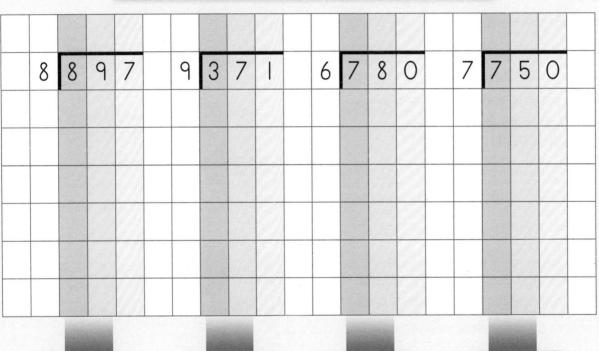

8 | 8 9 7   9 | 3 7 1   6 | 7 8 0   7 | 7 5 0

Check: Check: Check: Check:

Lesson 10.7

Review 👤 Find the perimeter or area.

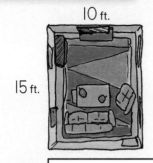

10 ft.

15 ft.

Area: _____

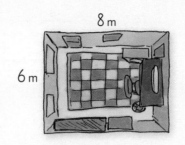

8 m

6 m

Area: _____

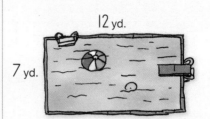

12 yd.

7 yd.

Perimeter: _____

Write each number in the place-value chart.

thousands	hundreds	tens	ones	
1	6	0		16 tens
				16 hundreds
				30 tens
				30 hundreds
				90 hundreds
				100 tens

Round each number to the underlined place.

29,001 ≈ _____

29,499 ≈ _____

29,500 ≈ _____

29,999 ≈ _____

Complete.

150 × 2 = _____

250 × 2 = _____

350 × 2 = _____

450 × 2 = _____

550 × 2 = _____

1,500 × 2 = _____

2,500 × 2 = _____

3,500 × 2 = _____

4,500 × 2 = _____

5,500 × 2 = _____

Lesson Activities 👥

A

1. Divide

2. Multiply

3. Subtract

4. Bring down the next digit (if needed)

Repeat (if needed)

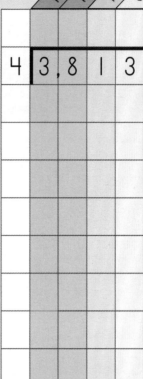

	thousands	hundreds	tens	ones
4	3,	8	1	3

B

Guess the Quotient!

2	3,	1	3	8		5	2,	5	4	6		3	6,	4	7	0

500

1,000

1,500

2,000

Practice

Circle the more accurate estimate for each quotient.

$3\overline{)62}$

20	30

$2\overline{)97}$

40	50

$6\overline{)71}$

10	20

$5\overline{)538}$

100	200

$4\overline{)193}$

50	60

$8\overline{)653}$

80	800

$6\overline{)7,345}$

1,000	2,000

$8\overline{)1,866}$

200	300

$5\overline{)3,070}$

600	6,000

Complete the words in the steps for long division.
Then, follow the steps to complete the problems.

1. D _____

2. M _____

3. S _____

4. B _____

6	7,	3	4	5		8	1,	8	6	6		5	3,	0	7	0

Review

Write whether each angle is acute, right, obtuse, or straight.

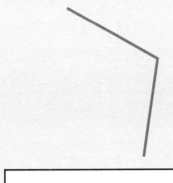

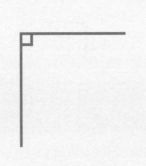

Complete. Convert your answer to a whole number or mixed number if possible.

$\frac{7}{10} + \frac{4}{10} =$ ☐ = ☐

$\frac{8}{5} - \frac{1}{5} =$ ☐ = ☐

$9 \times \frac{1}{2} =$ ☐ = ☐

$6 \times \frac{4}{5} =$ ☐ = ☐

Use a ruler to draw a line with the given length.

4 cm

4 mm

44 mm

Complete.

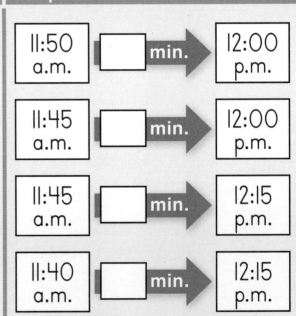

11:50 a.m.	☐ min.	12:00 p.m.
11:45 a.m.	☐ min.	12:00 p.m.
11:45 a.m.	☐ min.	12:15 p.m.
11:40 a.m.	☐ min.	12:15 p.m.

Lesson Activities 👥

_____ has
BOY'S NAME

4,073 _____ .
OBJECTS

He splits them into 3 equal groups.

- How many are in each group?

- How many are left over?

_____ has
GIRL'S NAME

1,925 _____ .
COLLECTIBLE ITEMS

She puts 4 on each shelf.

- How many shelves does she fill?

- How many are left over?

_____ has
BOY'S NAME

2,539 _____ .
BAKED GOODS

He puts 5 in each box.

- How many boxes does he fill?

- How many are left over?

_____ has
GIRL'S NAME

3,740 _____ of yarn.
UNITS OF LENGTH

She cuts the yarn into 2 equal pieces.

- How long is each piece?

- How much yarn is left over?

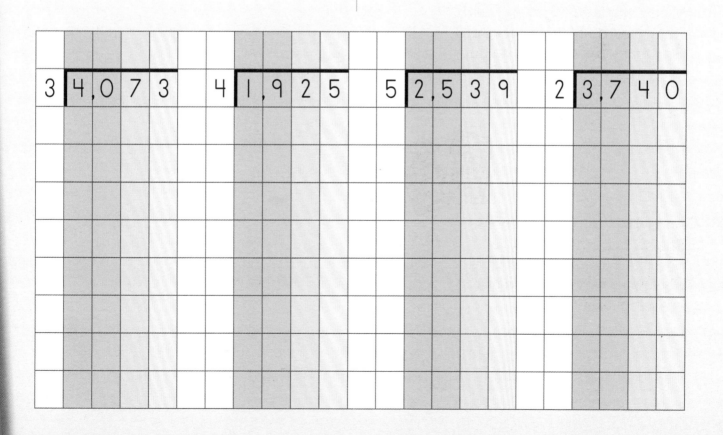

| 3 | 4,0 | 7 | 3 | | 4 | 1,9 | 2 | 5 | | 5 | 2,5 | 3 | 9 | | 2 | 3,7 | 4 | 0 |

Practice

Use long division to solve.
Write the long division problems in the work space.

Tarin has 974 rubber ducks. She packs 8 ducks in each package.

- How many packages does she fill?

- How many ducks are left over?

Aiden has 3,031 watermelons. He divides the watermelons as equally as possible into 5 boxes. How many watermelons are in each box?

Manny wants 2,650 trading cards. Trading cards come in packs of 6. How many packs should he buy?

Anna fills 1,467 water balloons. She splits them as evenly as possible into 4 big buckets. How many water balloons are in each bucket?

WORK SPACE

Review 👤 Use a protractor to measure the angles.

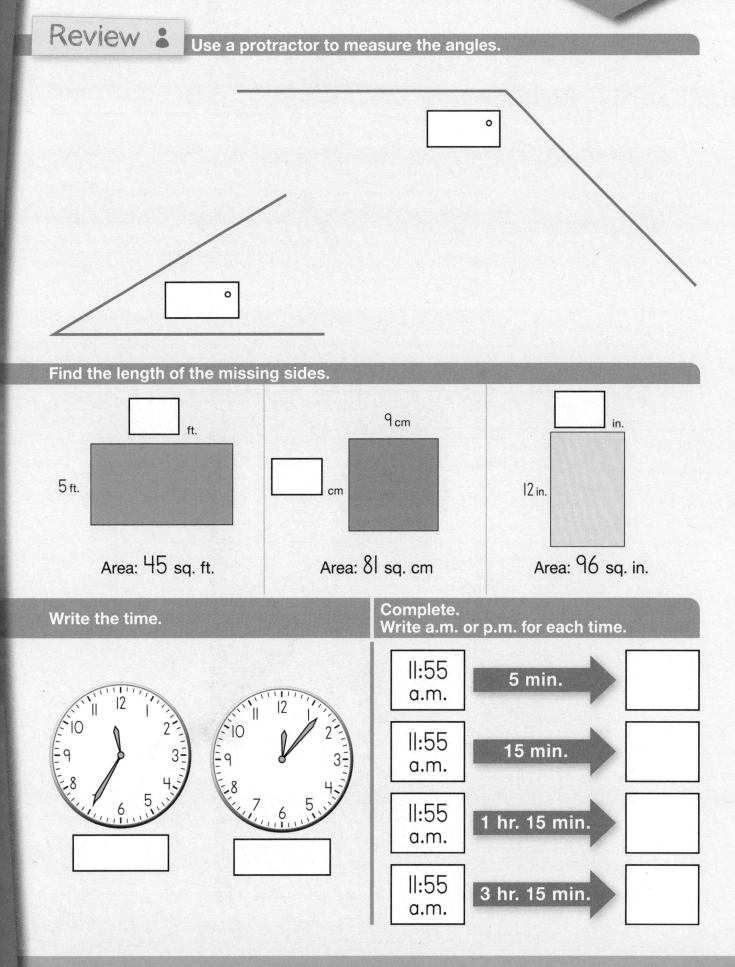

Find the length of the missing sides.

ft.

5 ft.

Area: 45 sq. ft.

9 cm

cm

Area: 81 sq. cm

in.

12 in.

Area: 96 sq. in.

Write the time.

Complete.
Write a.m. or p.m. for each time.

11:55 a.m.	5 min. →	
11:55 a.m.	15 min. →	
11:55 a.m.	1 hr. 15 min. →	
11:55 a.m.	3 hr. 15 min. →	

Unit Wrap-Up 👤

Write the steps for long division in order.

1. _____

2. _____

3. _____

4. _____

Circle the more accurate estimate for each division problem.

4 ⟌ 167 → | 30 | 40 |

5 ⟌ 614 → | 100 | 200 |

6 ⟌ 1,236 → | 200 | 2,000 |

Use long division to complete.
Then, multiply (or multiply and add) to check your answer.

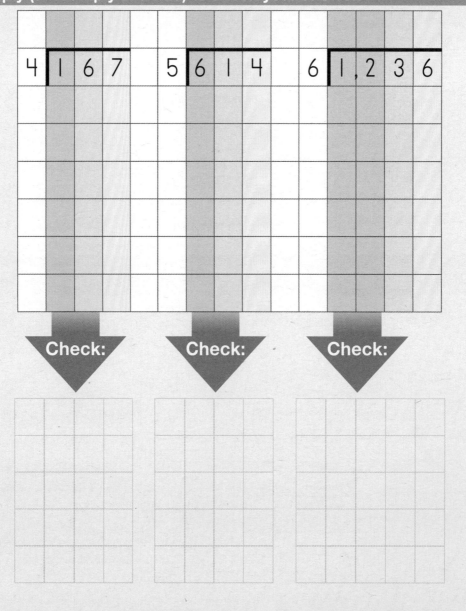

4 ⟌ 1 6 7   5 ⟌ 6 1 4   6 ⟌ 1,2 3 6

Check: Check: Check:

Unit Wrap-Up 👤

Jonah is a florist. He has 236 roses. He divides them as equally as possible into 9 vases. How many flowers are in each vase?

Olivia needs 180 plates for her new restaurant. Plates come in packs of 8. How many packs should she buy?

Caroline makes popcorn at the movie theater. She uses 3 cups of kernels for each batch. She has 478 cups of kernels. How many batches can she make?

Lucas has 1,080 grams of pizza dough. He splits the dough into 4 equal parts. How much does each part weigh?

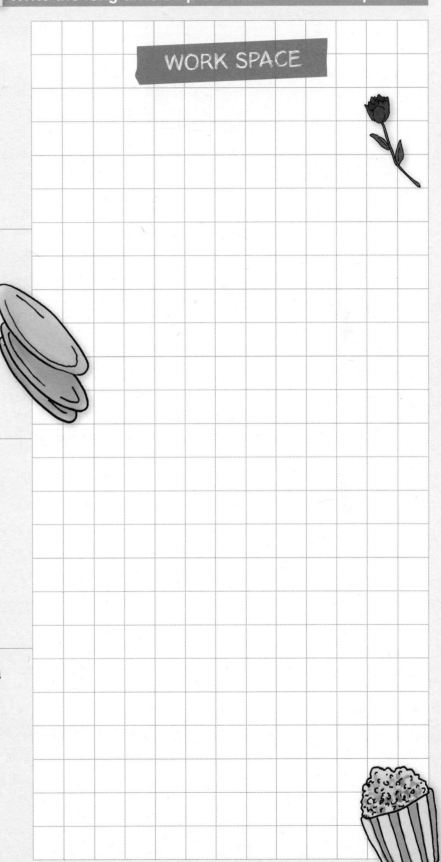

WORK SPACE

Lesson Activities 👥

A **point** marks a specific location.

• R

point R

YOU ARE HERE!

A **line** is a straight line that connects two points. It has no endpoints.

E   F

$\overleftrightarrow{EF}$

A **line segment** is part of a line. It has two endpoints.

A   B

$\overline{AB}$

A **ray** is part of a line. It has one endpoint.

X   Y

$\overrightarrow{XY}$

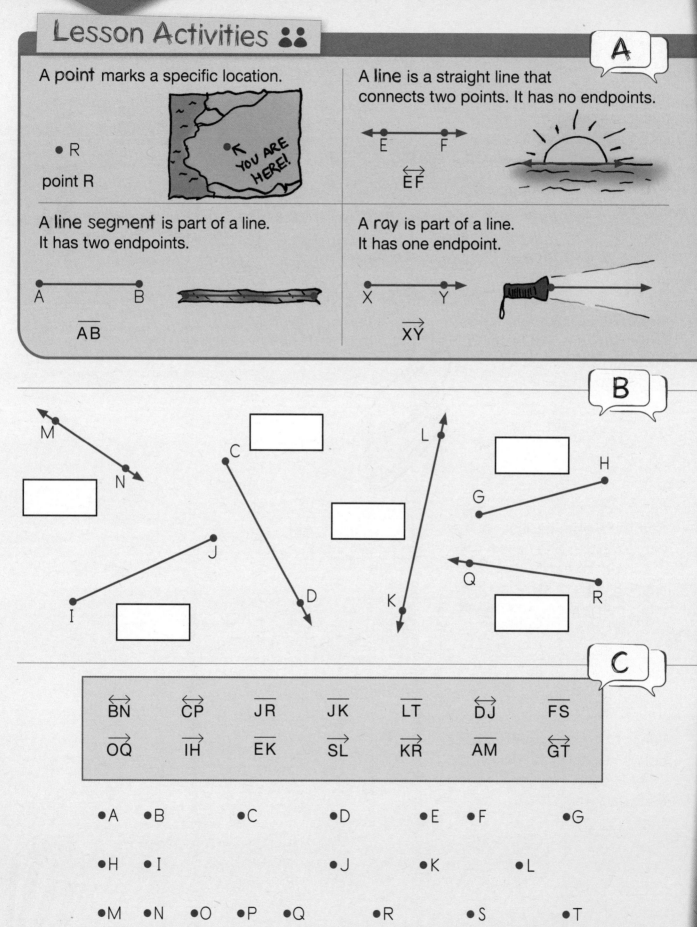

$\overleftrightarrow{BN}$	$\overleftrightarrow{CP}$	$\overline{JR}$	$\overline{JK}$	$\overline{LT}$	$\overleftrightarrow{DJ}$	$\overline{FS}$
$\overrightarrow{OQ}$	$\overrightarrow{IH}$	$\overline{EK}$	$\overrightarrow{SL}$	$\overrightarrow{KR}$	$\overline{AM}$	$\overleftrightarrow{GT}$

•A   •B   •C   •D   •E •F   •G

•H   •I   •J   •K   •L

•M •N   •O •P •Q   •R   •S   •T

Practice 👤 Match.

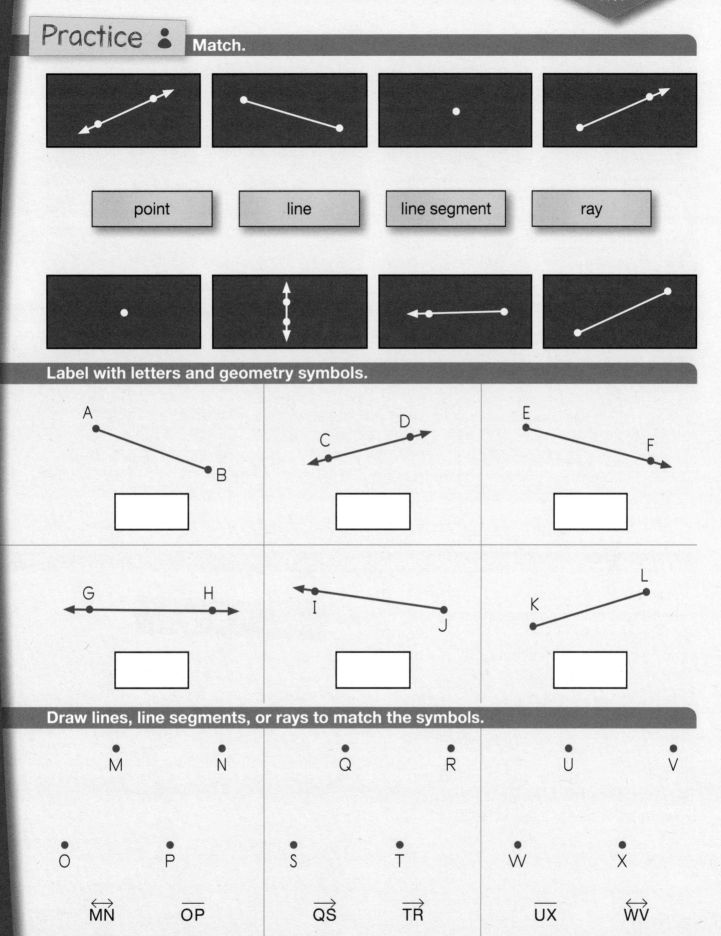

point   line   line segment   ray

Label with letters and geometry symbols.

Draw lines, line segments, or rays to match the symbols.

$\overleftrightarrow{MN}$ $\overline{OP}$ $\overrightarrow{QS}$ $\overrightarrow{TR}$ $\overline{UX}$ $\overleftrightarrow{WV}$

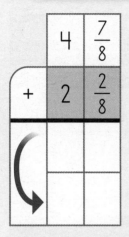

Review 👤 Complete.

$$4 \frac{7}{8}$$
$$+ \ 2 \frac{2}{8}$$

$$3 \frac{5}{10}$$
$$+ \ 4 \frac{5}{10}$$

$$3 \frac{2}{3}$$
$$- \ 1 \frac{1}{3}$$

$$5 \frac{1}{4}$$
$$- \ 2 \frac{3}{4}$$

Complete.

6 km = [ ] m

6 km 172 m = [ ] m

8 cm = [ ] mm

8 cm 5 mm = [ ] mm

5 m = [ ] cm

5 m 8 cm = [ ] cm

7 ft. = [ ] in.

7 ft. 6 in. = [ ] in.

Solve. Write your equations in the work space.

Levi buys 6 tickets to a show.
Each ticket costs the same amount.
He spends $228.
How much does each ticket cost?

WORK SPACE

4 friends work together to earn $188.
They divide the money evenly.
How much does each friend get?

Lesson 11.1

Lesson Activities 👥

A

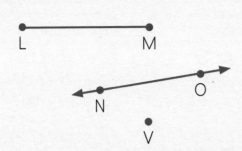
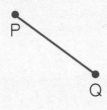
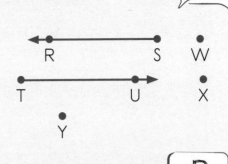

B

Parallel lines
are always the same distance apart.

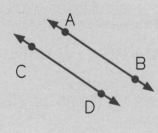

$\overleftrightarrow{AB}$ ‖ $\overleftrightarrow{CD}$

Intersecting lines
cross each other.

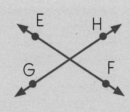

$\overleftrightarrow{EF}$ intersects $\overleftrightarrow{GH}$

Perpendicular lines
intersect to form 4 right angles.

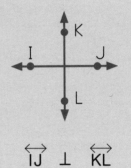

$\overleftrightarrow{IJ}$ ⊥ $\overleftrightarrow{KL}$

C

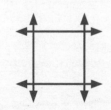

☐ pair(s) of parallel sides

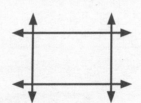

☐ pair(s) of parallel sides

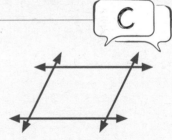

☐ pair(s) of parallel sides

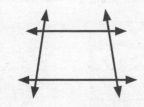

☐ pair(s) of parallel sides

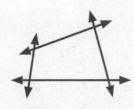

☐ pair(s) of parallel sides

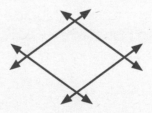

☐ pair(s) of parallel sides

11.2

Practice

Circle **T** if the statement is true.
Circle **F** if the statement is false.

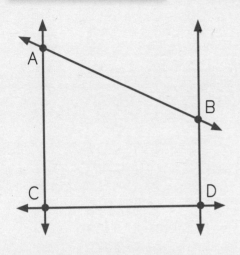

$\overleftrightarrow{AC} \parallel \overleftrightarrow{BD}$ **T** **F**	$\overleftrightarrow{AB} \parallel \overleftrightarrow{CD}$ **T** **F**
$\overleftrightarrow{AC} \perp \overleftrightarrow{CD}$ **T** **F**	$\overleftrightarrow{AC} \perp \overleftrightarrow{AB}$ **T** **F**
$\overleftrightarrow{BD} \perp \overleftrightarrow{AB}$ **T** **F**	$\overleftrightarrow{BD} \perp \overleftrightarrow{CD}$ **T** **F**

Draw a quadrilateral to match each description.

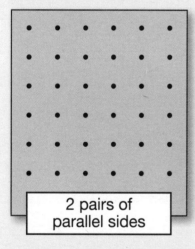

2 pairs of
parallel sides

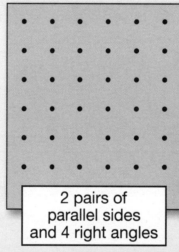

2 pairs of
parallel sides
and 4 right angles

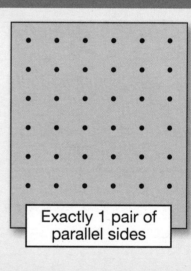

Exactly 1 pair of
parallel sides

Use the clues to label the streets.

- Pine is parallel to Maple.

- Oak is perpendicular to
  Maple and Pine.

- Elm intersects Maple, Pine,
  and Oak.

Lesson 11.2

Review

Color the circles to match the fractions.

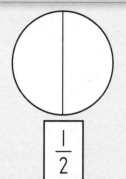 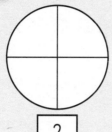 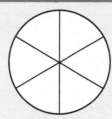 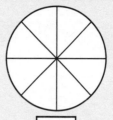 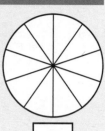

$\dfrac{1}{2}$ $\dfrac{2}{4}$ $\dfrac{3}{6}$ $\dfrac{4}{8}$ $\dfrac{5}{10}$

Complete the missing numbers.

$7 \times \boxed{} = 42$

$6 \times \boxed{} = 30$

$9 \times \boxed{} = 81$

$63 \div \boxed{} = 9$

$54 \div \boxed{} = 6$

$49 \div \boxed{} = 7$

Use long division to solve.

$4\overline{)728}$ $2\overline{)728}$

Solve. Write the equations you use.

Kiah uses 2 boards to build a storage box.
One board is $1\frac{2}{10}$ m long.
The other board is $1\frac{5}{10}$ m long.
What is the total length of both boards?

John's shoe is $8\frac{3}{4}$ in. long.
His dad's shoe is $11\frac{1}{4}$ in. long.
How much shorter is John's shoe than his
dad's shoe?

Lesson Activities 👥

A

Quadrilaterals
have 4 sides.

Parallelograms
have 2 pairs of
parallel sides.

Trapezoids
have exactly 1 pair of
parallel sides.

Rectangles
have 4 right angles.

Squares
have 4 right angles
and 4 equal sides.

Rhombuses
have 4 equal sides and
2 pairs of parallel sides.

B

Quadrilaterals	Parallelograms	Trapezoids
Rectangles	Squares	Rhombuses

C

Quadrilateral Capture

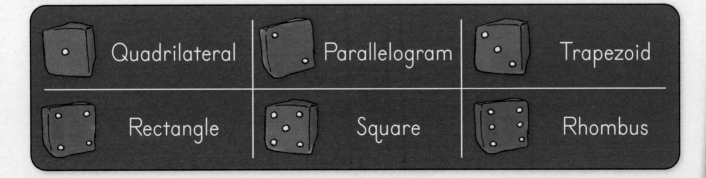

Practice

Use the key to color the shapes.
Some of the shapes will have more than one pattern.

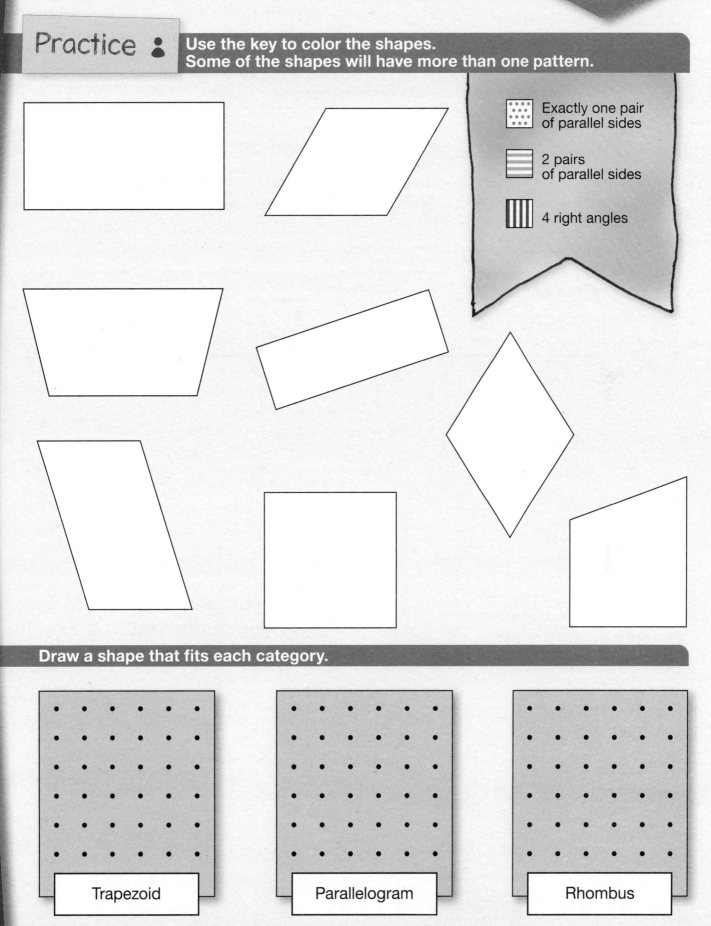

Key:
- Exactly one pair of parallel sides
- 2 pairs of parallel sides
- 4 right angles

Draw a shape that fits each category.

Trapezoid

Parallelogram

Rhombus

Review

Convert the fractions to mixed numbers or whole numbers.
Convert the mixed numbers to fractions.

$\frac{80}{10}$ = ▢

$\frac{16}{3}$ = ▢

$\frac{32}{5}$ = ▢

$5\frac{5}{6}$ = ▢

$8\frac{1}{3}$ = ▢

$9\frac{1}{2}$ = ▢

Use long division to solve.

6 ⟌ 7 9   6 ⟌ 7 3   6 ⟌ 6 7   6 ⟌ 6 1   6 ⟌ 5 5

Solve. Write your equations in the work space.

The hotel costs $179 per night. How much does it cost to stay at the hotel for 6 nights?

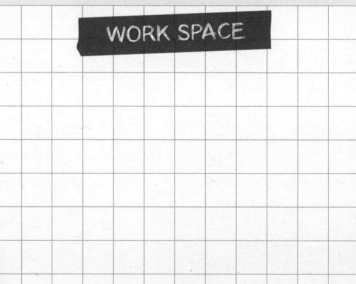

WORK SPACE

There are 187 beds at the hotel. There are 4 pillows on each bed. How many pillows are there on the beds in all?

Lesson Activities 👥

Rectangles

4 sides
Exactly 1 pair of parallel sides
2 pairs of parallel sides
4 right angles
4 equal sides

Quadrilaterals

 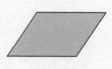 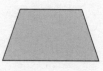

4 sides
Exactly 1 pair of parallel sides
2 pairs of parallel sides
4 right angles
4 equal sides

Squares

4 sides
Exactly 1 pair of parallel sides
2 pairs of parallel sides
4 right angles
4 equal sides

Rhombuses

 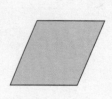 

4 sides
Exactly 1 pair of parallel sides
2 pairs of parallel sides
4 right angles
4 equal sides

Parallelograms

4 sides
Exactly 1 pair of parallel sides
2 pairs of parallel sides
4 right angles
4 equal sides

Trapezoids

 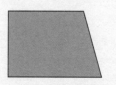

4 sides
Exactly 1 pair of parallel sides
2 pairs of parallel sides
4 right angles
4 equal sides

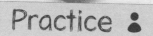

Practice

Follow the directions for each group of shapes.

Circle the parallelograms.
X the shapes that are not parallelograms.

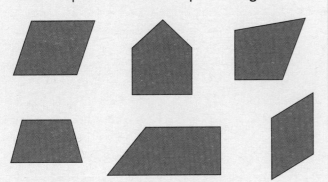

Circle the trapezoids.
X the shapes that are not trapezoids.

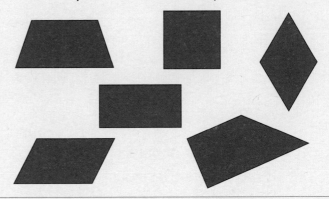

Circle the rectangles.
X the shapes that are not rectangles.

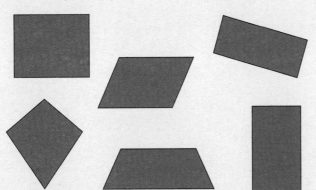

Circle the squares.
X the shapes that are not squares.

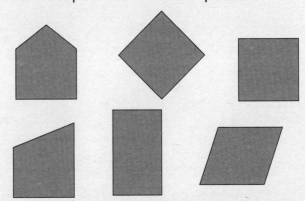

Use the key to color the robot. Use the most specific name possible for each shape.

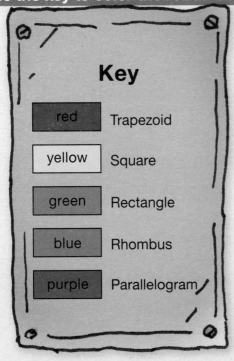

Key

red	Trapezoid
yellow	Square
green	Rectangle
blue	Rhombus
purple	Parallelogram

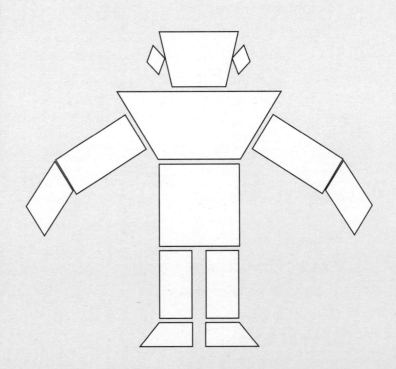

Review

Write whether each angle is acute, right, obtuse, or straight.

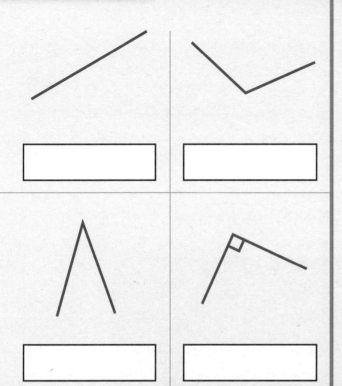

Complete.

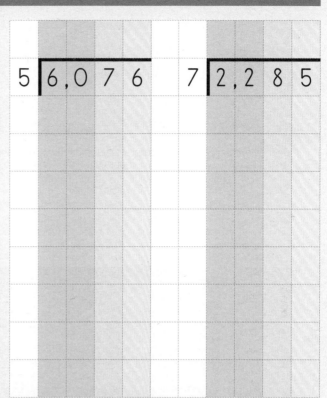

Solve. Write the equations you use.

The square poster has a perimeter of 92 inches.
How long is each side?

The rug is 3 feet wide.
It has an area of 51 square feet.
How long is the rug?

3 ft.

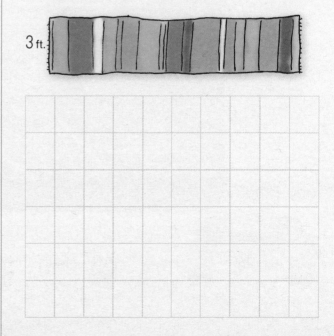

Lesson Activities 👥

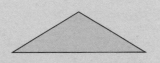

Right triangles
have 1 right angle.

Obtuse triangles
have 1 obtuse angle.

Acute triangles
have 3 acute angles.

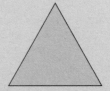

Triangle Four in a Row

Key					
Acute triangle	Right triangle	Obtuse triangle	Lose your turn	Wild	Remove one counter

Practice 👤 Match.

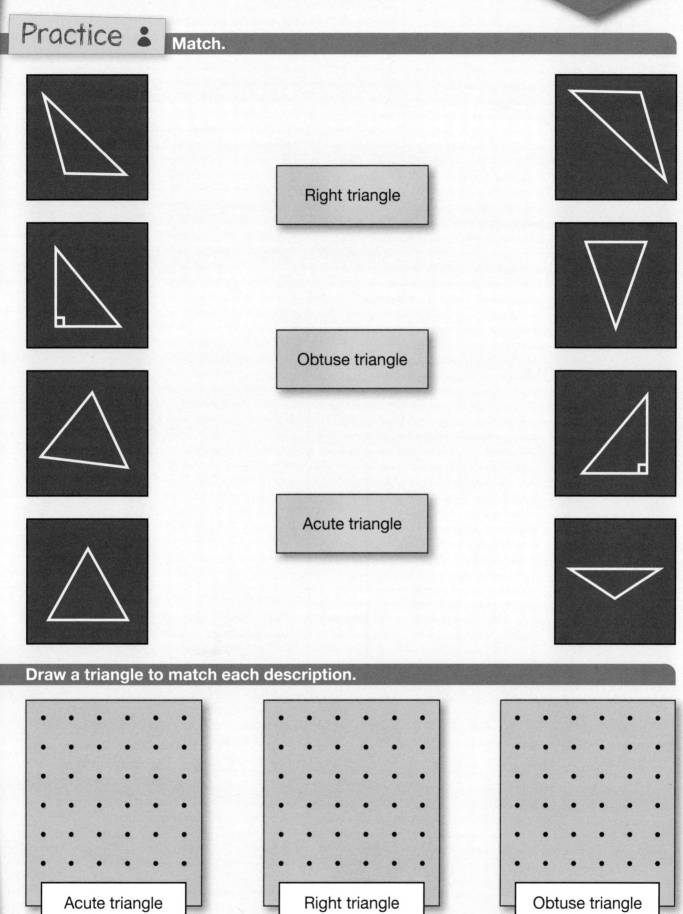

Right triangle

Obtuse triangle

Acute triangle

Draw a triangle to match each description.

Acute triangle

Right triangle

Obtuse triangle

Review 👤 Label with letters and geometry symbols.

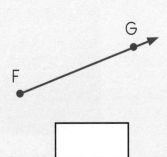

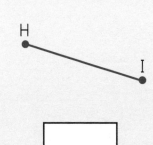

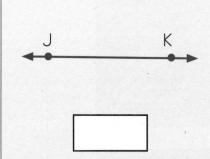

Complete. Convert your answer to a whole number or mixed number if possible.

$7 \times \dfrac{1}{5} = \boxed{\dfrac{7}{5}} = \boxed{1\dfrac{2}{5}}$

$7 \times \dfrac{2}{5} = \boxed{} = \boxed{}$

$7 \times \dfrac{3}{5} = \boxed{} = \boxed{}$

$7 \times \dfrac{4}{5} = \boxed{} = \boxed{}$

$7 \times \dfrac{5}{5} = \boxed{} = \boxed{}$

Complete.

	3	0	7
×			6

	4	3	9
×			8

	7	3	0
×			7

	7	0	3
×			7

Solve. Write the equations you use.

Nicole runs 3 km 400 m. She stops and takes a rest. Then, she runs 2 km 850 m farther. How far does she run in all?

Camden has a ribbon that is 1 meter long. He cuts the ribbon into 5 equal pieces. How long is each piece in centimeters?

Lesson Activities 👥

B

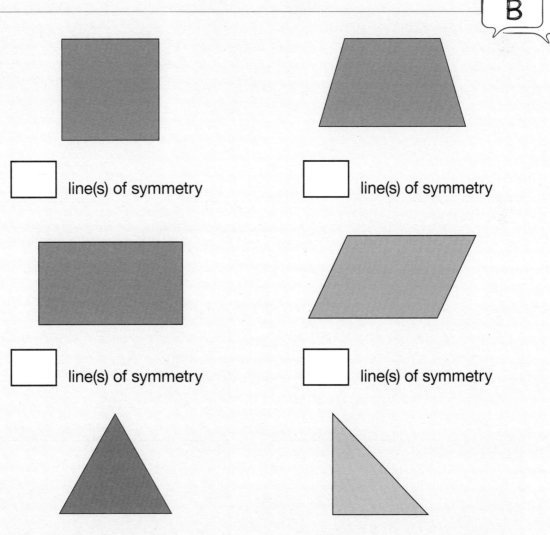

Practice 👤 Is the dotted line a line of symmetry for the shape? Write yes or no.

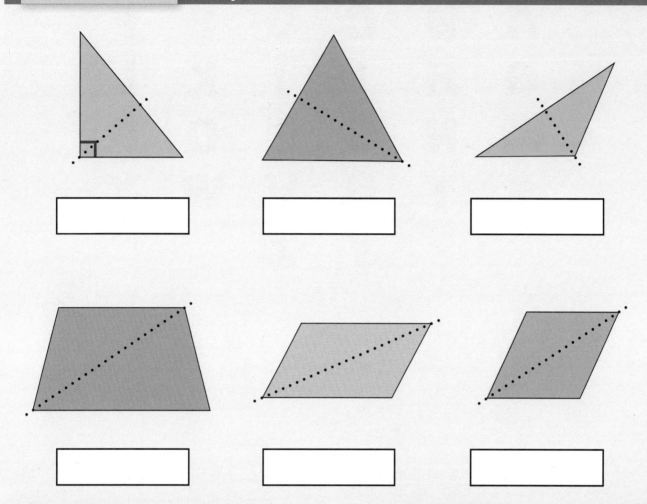

Draw the missing halves for these symmetric shapes.

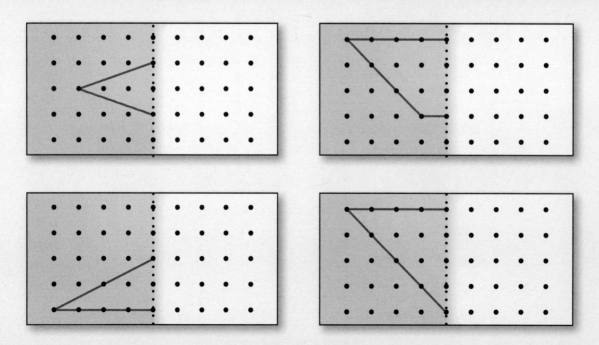

Lesson 11.6

Review 👤 Measure each line to the nearest quarter-inch.

in.

in.

in.

| Complete. | Use long division to solve. |

9 ft. = ☐ yd.

9 ft. = ☐ in.

72 in. = ☐ ft.

⭐ 72 in. = ☐ yd.

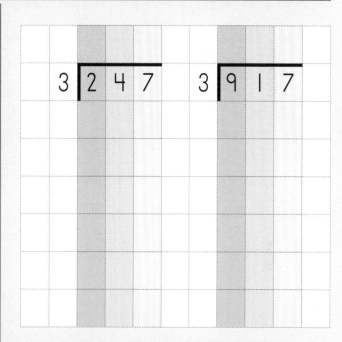

$3\overline{)247}$ $3\overline{)917}$

Solve. Write the equations you use.

Elyse's family has $2\frac{3}{8}$ pies left after a party.
Each pie is cut into eighths.
How many slices of pie do they have?

Each batch of granola requires $\frac{2}{3}$ cup of
dried fruit. How much dried fruit do you
need to make 4 batches?

Unit Wrap-Up 👤 **Match.**

  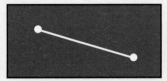 

point	line	ray	line segment

**Use the diagram to tell whether each statement is true or false.
Circle T if the statement is true. Circle F if the statement is false.**

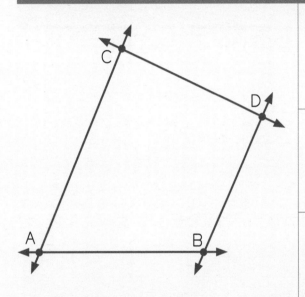

$\overleftrightarrow{AC} \parallel \overleftrightarrow{BD}$	$\overleftrightarrow{AC} \parallel \overleftrightarrow{CD}$
T **F**	**T** **F**
$\overleftrightarrow{AC} \parallel \overleftrightarrow{AB}$	$\overleftrightarrow{AB}$ intersects $\overleftrightarrow{BD}$
T **F**	**T** **F**
$\overleftrightarrow{AB} \perp \overleftrightarrow{BD}$	$\overleftrightarrow{BD} \perp \overleftrightarrow{CD}$
T **F**	**T** **F**

Complete.

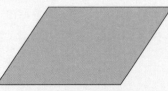

▢ pair(s) of parallel sides	▢ pair(s) of parallel sides	▢ pair(s) of parallel sides
▢ right angle(s)	▢ right angle(s)	▢ right angle(s)

Unit Wrap-Up

Use the words in the word bank to label each shape. Use the most specific name possible for each shape. You will use each word once.

acute triangle	quadrilateral	square
right triangle	trapezoid	rectangle
obtuse triangle	parallelogram	rhombus

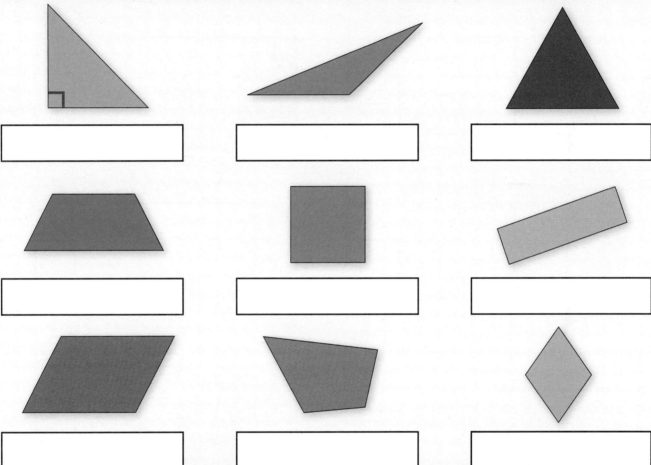

Draw as many lines of symmetry as possible for each shape.

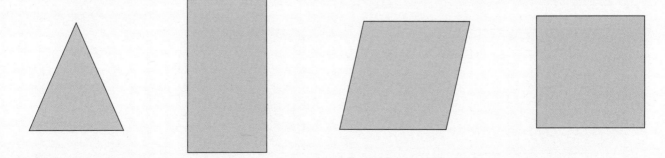

Lesson Activities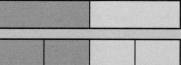

A

Equivalent Fractions have the same value but look different from each other.

$$\frac{1}{2} = \boxed{}$$

B

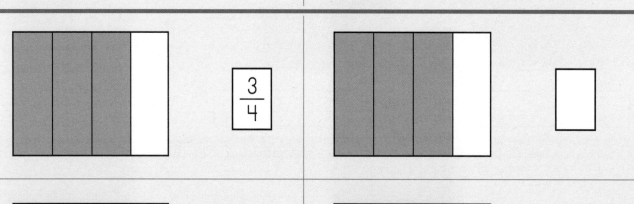

$$\frac{1}{3}$$

$$\frac{3}{4}$$

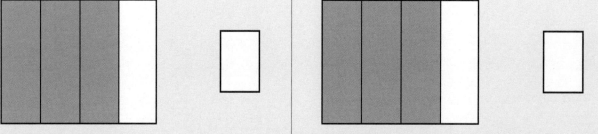

Practice

Follow the directions. Then, answer the questions.

The granola bar is cut into thirds. Draw lines to divide each third into 2 equal parts.

How many parts are there now? ___

The granola bar is cut into thirds. Draw lines to divide each third into 3 equal parts.

How many parts are there now? ___

The granola bar is cut into halves. Draw lines to divide each half into 4 equal parts.

How many parts are there now? ___

The granola bar is cut into fourths. Draw lines to divide each fourth into 2 equal parts.

How many parts are there now? ___

$\frac{1}{3}$ of the pizza has pepperoni. Draw lines to divide each third into 3 equal slices.

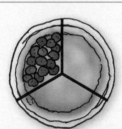

What fraction of the pizza has pepperoni now? ___

$\frac{3}{4}$ of the pizza has mushrooms. Draw lines to divide each fourth into 2 equal slices.

What fraction of the pizza has mushrooms now? ___

The cake is cut into sixths. Draw lines to divide each sixth into 2 equal slices.

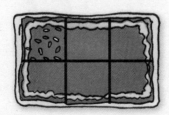

What fraction of the cake has sprinkles now? ___

The cake is cut into fifths. Draw lines to divide each fifth into 3 equal slices.

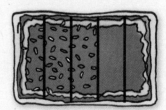

What fraction of the cake has sprinkles now? ___

Review

Choose the more reasonable measurement for each angle.

90°	95°

30°	70°

125°	165°

Complete.

$6 \times 90 = $ ____

$7 \times 80 = $ ____

$8 \times 90 = $ ____

$6 \times 900 = $ ____

$7 \times 800 = $ ____

$8 \times 900 = $ ____

Complete. Write a.m. or p.m. for each time.

11:15 a.m. → 1 hr. → ____

11:15 a.m. → 2 hr. → ____

10:30 a.m. → 3 hr. → ____

10:30 a.m. → 4 hr. → ____

Solve. Write the equations you use.

Emilia's mom bought 3 sunhats, 2 bottles of sunscreen, and 4 water bottles. How much did she spend?

Sunhat $17

Sunscreen $14

Water bottle ... $19

Lesson Activities 👥

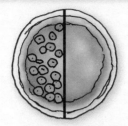 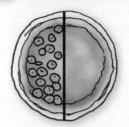 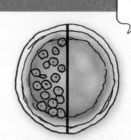

$\dfrac{1}{2}$ = ☐ $\dfrac{1}{2}$ = ☐ $\dfrac{1}{2}$ = ☐

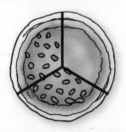 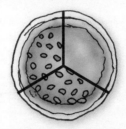 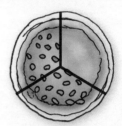

$\dfrac{2}{3}$ = ☐ $\dfrac{2}{3}$ = ☐ $\dfrac{2}{3}$ = ☐

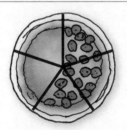 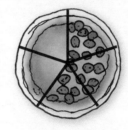 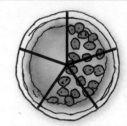

$\dfrac{3}{5}$ = ☐ $\dfrac{3}{5}$ = ☐ $\dfrac{3}{5}$ = ☐

$\dfrac{1}{2}$ 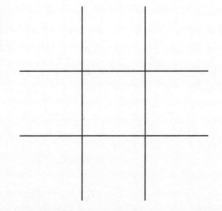 $\dfrac{3}{4}$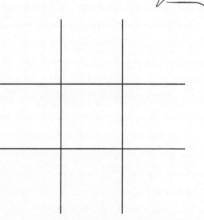

Practice

Complete the equivalent fractions. Use the multiplier shown.

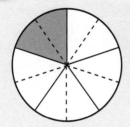

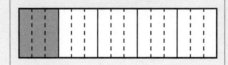

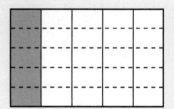

$\frac{1}{5} \; \overset{\times 2}{\underset{\times 2}{=}} \; \boxed{\frac{2}{10}}$

$\frac{1}{5} \; \overset{\times 3}{\underset{\times 3}{=}} \; \boxed{\frac{3}{15}}$

$\frac{1}{5} \; \overset{\times 5}{\underset{\times 5}{=}} \; \boxed{\frac{5}{25}}$

$\frac{2}{5} = \boxed{}$

$\frac{2}{5} = \boxed{}$

$\frac{2}{5} = \boxed{}$

$\frac{3}{5} = \boxed{}$

$\frac{3}{5} = \boxed{}$

$\frac{3}{5} = \boxed{}$

$\frac{4}{5} = \boxed{}$

$\frac{4}{5} = \boxed{}$

$\frac{4}{5} = \boxed{}$

$\frac{5}{5} = \boxed{}$

$\frac{5}{5} = \boxed{}$

$\frac{5}{5} = \boxed{}$

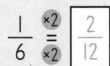

$\frac{1}{6} \; \overset{\times 2}{\underset{\times 2}{=}} \; \boxed{\frac{2}{12}}$

$\frac{2}{6} = \boxed{}$

$\frac{3}{6} = \boxed{}$

$\frac{4}{6} = \boxed{}$

$\frac{5}{6} = \boxed{}$

$\frac{6}{6} = \boxed{}$

Review

Complete.

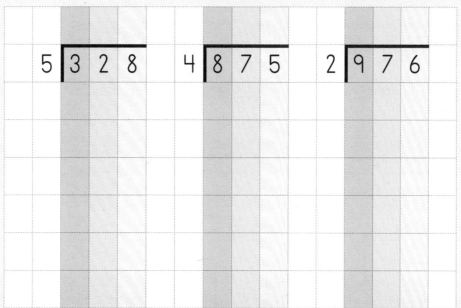

5	3	2	8	4	8	7	5	2	9	7	6

Use a ruler to draw a line with the given length.

5 cm

5 mm

55 mm

Find all possible factor pairs for each number.

Factor pairs of 14

Factor pairs of 28

Use the diagram to answer the questions.

What is the area of the dining room?

What is the area of the living room?

What is the total area of both rooms?

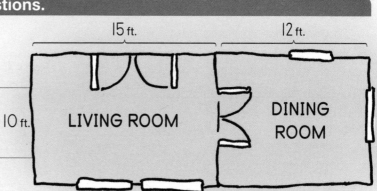

15 ft.   12 ft.

10 ft.   LIVING ROOM   DINING ROOM

12.3

Lesson Activities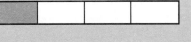

$\dfrac{1}{4} = \dfrac{\boxed{}}{8}$

$\dfrac{2}{3} = \dfrac{\boxed{10}}{}$

$\dfrac{5}{6} = \dfrac{\boxed{}}{12}$

$\dfrac{1}{2} = \dfrac{\boxed{5}}{}$

$\dfrac{7}{8} = \dfrac{\boxed{14}}{}$

Fill the Fractions

$\dfrac{3}{8} = \dfrac{\boxed{6}}{}$

$\dfrac{1}{4} = \dfrac{\boxed{}}{24}$

$\dfrac{1}{3} = \dfrac{\boxed{}}{15}$

$\dfrac{3}{6} = \dfrac{\boxed{}}{18}$

$\dfrac{1}{2} = \dfrac{\boxed{}}{22}$

$\dfrac{3}{10} = \dfrac{\boxed{}}{20}$

$\dfrac{7}{10} = \dfrac{\boxed{21}}{}$

$\dfrac{4}{5} = \dfrac{\boxed{12}}{}$

$\dfrac{1}{5} = \dfrac{\boxed{}}{15}$

$\dfrac{2}{3} = \dfrac{\boxed{8}}{}$

$\dfrac{2}{6} = \dfrac{\boxed{10}}{}$

$\dfrac{3}{4} = \dfrac{\boxed{}}{8}$

Practice 👤 Use the pictures to complete the equivalent fractions.

$$\frac{3}{4} \, \substack{\times 3 \\ = \\ \times 3} \, \frac{}{12}$$

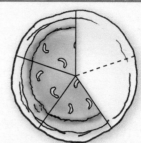

$$\frac{3}{5} = \frac{9}{}$$

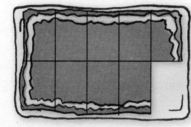

$$\frac{9}{10} = \frac{18}{}$$

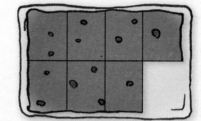

$$\frac{7}{8} = \frac{14}{}$$

The quilt is split into 16 triangles. Each triangle is $\frac{1}{16}$ of the quilt. Complete the equivalent fractions. Then, use the key to color the quilt. You may color it with any design that matches the fractions.

$$\frac{1}{4} = \frac{}{16} \qquad \frac{1}{8} = \frac{}{16} \qquad \frac{3}{8} = \frac{}{16}$$

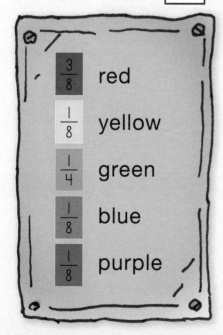

$\frac{3}{8}$ red

$\frac{1}{8}$ yellow

$\frac{1}{4}$ green

$\frac{1}{8}$ blue

$\frac{1}{8}$ purple

12.3

Review

Label with letters and geometry symbols.

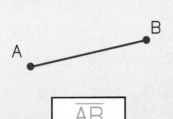

$$\overline{AB}$$

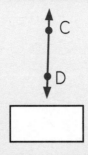

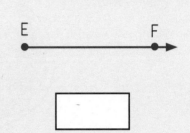

Complete.	Complete.

3,509 × 7

6,843 × 4

6 weeks = [   ] days

6 weeks, 3 days = [   ] days

63 days = [   ] weeks

68 days = [   ] weeks, [   ] days

Solve. Write your equations in the work space.

A one-day ticket to the theme park costs $119. How much does it cost to buy 4 tickets?

WORK SPACE

If you buy a ticket for more than one day, you get a discount. A three-day ticket to the theme park costs $288. How much does each day cost?

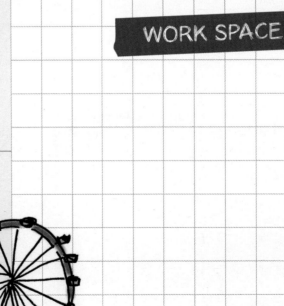

Lesson Activities 👥

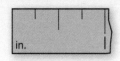 $\dfrac{1}{2} = \dfrac{\boxed{}}{4}$

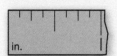 $\dfrac{1}{4} = \dfrac{\boxed{}}{8}$ $\dfrac{1}{2} = \dfrac{\boxed{}}{8}$ $\dfrac{3}{4} = \dfrac{\boxed{}}{8}$

$\dfrac{1}{4} = \dfrac{\boxed{}}{16}$ $\dfrac{1}{2} = \dfrac{\boxed{}}{16}$ $\dfrac{3}{4} = \dfrac{\boxed{}}{16}$

$\dfrac{1}{8} = \dfrac{\boxed{}}{16}$ $\dfrac{3}{8} = \dfrac{\boxed{}}{16}$ $\dfrac{5}{8} = \dfrac{\boxed{}}{16}$ $\dfrac{7}{8} = \dfrac{\boxed{}}{16}$

 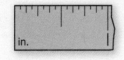 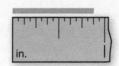 

$\dfrac{5}{16}$ in. $\dfrac{5}{8}$ in.   in.   in.

Fraction War

Fraction War	2 $\dfrac{3}{16}$	3 $\dfrac{11}{16}$	4 $\dfrac{7}{16}$
5 $\dfrac{3}{8}$	6 $\dfrac{1}{4}$	7 $\dfrac{1}{2}$	8 $\dfrac{3}{4}$
9 $\dfrac{5}{8}$	10 $\dfrac{9}{16}$	11 $\dfrac{5}{16}$	12 $\dfrac{13}{16}$

Practice 👤

Use a ruler to draw lines that match each length.
Then, write <, >, or = to complete the fractions.

$\frac{3}{4}$ in.

$\frac{3}{8}$ in.

$\frac{3}{16}$ in.

$\frac{9}{16}$ in.

$\frac{7}{8}$ in.

$\frac{7}{16}$ in.

$\frac{3}{4}$ ◯ $\frac{3}{8}$

$\frac{3}{8}$ ◯ $\frac{3}{16}$

$\frac{3}{16}$ ◯ $\frac{3}{4}$

$\frac{9}{16}$ ◯ $\frac{7}{8}$

$\frac{7}{8}$ ◯ $\frac{7}{16}$

$\frac{3}{4}$ ◯ $\frac{7}{8}$

Use the printed rulers to measure the lines.

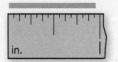

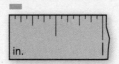

☐ in.

☐ in.

☐ in.

☐ in.

Complete the equivalent fractions.

$\frac{1}{2} = \frac{\boxed{}}{20}$

$\frac{7}{8} = \frac{\boxed{21}}{\boxed{}}$

$\frac{3}{4} = \frac{\boxed{}}{12}$

$\frac{3}{8} = \frac{\boxed{}}{40}$

$\frac{1}{8} = \frac{\boxed{}}{48}$

$\frac{1}{16} = \frac{\boxed{2}}{\boxed{}}$

Draw as many lines of symmetry as possible for each shape.

20 × 30 = ☐

40 × 40 = ☐

50 × 60 = ☐

80 × 50 = ☐

70 × 70 = ☐

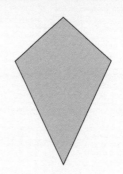 

 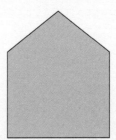

Use the clues to complete the chart.

- Leela scored 50 points.

- Mason scored 4 times as many points as Leela.

- Kit scored half as many points as Mason.

 • Mason scored half as many points as Noor.

Name	Points
Leela	
Mason	
Kit	
Noor	

Complete the boxes to solve.

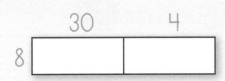

8 × 34 = ☐

6 × 92 = ☐

Lesson Activities

$$\frac{10}{100} \quad \frac{20}{100} \quad \frac{\boxed{}}{100} \quad \frac{40}{100} \quad \frac{50}{100} \quad \frac{\boxed{}}{100} \quad \frac{70}{100} \quad \frac{80}{100} \quad \frac{\boxed{}}{100} \quad \frac{100}{100}$$

$$\frac{1}{10} \quad \frac{2}{10} \quad \frac{3}{10} \quad \frac{\boxed{}}{10} \quad \frac{5}{10} \quad \frac{6}{10} \quad \frac{\boxed{}}{10} \quad \frac{8}{10} \quad \frac{9}{10} \quad \frac{10}{10}$$

B

$$\frac{7}{10} = \frac{\boxed{}}{100} \qquad \frac{5}{10} = \frac{\boxed{}}{100} \qquad \frac{4}{10} = \frac{\boxed{40}}{\boxed{}}$$

$$\frac{6}{10} = \boxed{\frac{60}{}} \qquad \frac{3}{10} = \frac{\boxed{}}{100} \qquad \frac{8}{10} = \boxed{\frac{80}{}}$$

C

Fraction War	2 $\frac{65}{100}$	3 $\frac{34}{100}$	4 $\frac{7}{10}$
5 $\frac{56}{100}$	6 $\frac{4}{10}$	7 $\frac{6}{10}$	8 $\frac{47}{100}$
9 $\frac{5}{10}$	10 $\frac{60}{100}$	11 $\frac{48}{100}$	12 $\frac{39}{100}$

Practice

**Complete the equivalent fractions.
Then, write <, >, or = to compare the fractions.**

$\frac{5}{10} = \frac{}{100}$ $\frac{6}{10} = \frac{}{100}$ $\frac{7}{10} = \frac{}{100}$

$\frac{8}{10} = \frac{}{100}$ $\frac{9}{10} = \frac{}{100}$ $\frac{10}{10} = \frac{}{100}$

$\frac{9}{10} \bigcirc \frac{80}{100}$ $\frac{5}{10} \bigcirc \frac{70}{100}$ $\frac{60}{100} \bigcirc \frac{7}{10}$

 $\frac{6}{10} \bigcirc \frac{63}{100}$ $\frac{8}{10} \bigcirc \frac{74}{100}$ $\frac{99}{100} \bigcirc \frac{10}{10}$

The grid is split into 100 squares. Each square is $\frac{1}{100}$ of the grid.
Complete the equivalent fractions. Then, use the key to color the grid.
You may color it with any design that matches the fractions.

red: $\frac{3}{10} = \frac{}{100}$

orange: $\frac{2}{10} = \frac{}{100}$

yellow: $\frac{1}{10} = \frac{}{100}$

blue: $\frac{4}{10} = \frac{}{100}$

Review 👤 Complete.

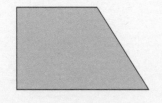

☐ pair(s) of
parallel sides

☐ right angle(s)

☐ pair(s) of
parallel sides

☐ right angle(s)

☐ pair(s) of
parallel sides

☐ right angle(s)

Circle the prime numbers.

11	12	13	14
15	16	17	18
19	20	21	22
23	24	25	26

Complete.

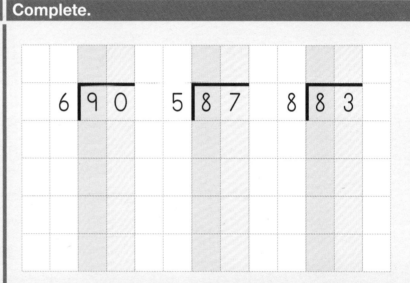

6) 9 0   5) 8 7   8) 8 3

Solve. Write the equations you use.

Arya mixes $2\frac{1}{3}$ liters of lemonade and
$\frac{2}{3}$ liter of pineapple juice to make punch.
How much more lemonade than pineapple
juice did she use?

A small bag of rice weighs $2\frac{5}{8}$ pounds. A
large bag of rice weighs $5\frac{7}{8}$ pounds.
What is the total weight of a small bag and
a large bag?

Lesson Activities 👥

A

$\frac{2}{5}$ ◯ $\frac{4}{5}$ $\frac{9}{10}$ ◯ $\frac{8}{10}$ $\frac{14}{16}$ ◯ $\frac{15}{16}$

B

Jeremy has $\frac{3}{4}$ cup of flour.
He needs $\frac{5}{8}$ cup to make muffins.
Does he have enough flour?

$\frac{5}{8}$ c. flour

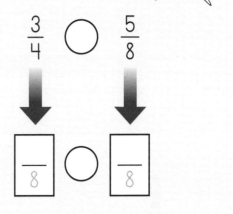

$\frac{3}{4}$ ◯ $\frac{5}{8}$

$\frac{}{8}$ ◯ $\frac{}{8}$

The purple ribbon is $\frac{7}{10}$ meter long.
The orange ribbon is $\frac{4}{5}$ meter long.
Which ribbon is longer?

RIBBON $\frac{7}{10}$ m

RIBBON $\frac{4}{5}$ m

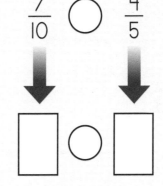

$\frac{7}{10}$ ◯ $\frac{4}{5}$

☐ ◯ ☐

C

Etta has $\frac{2}{3}$ kg of red modeling clay,
$\frac{5}{6}$ kg of blue modeling clay,
and $\frac{7}{12}$ kg of green modeling clay.
Which color does she have the least of?

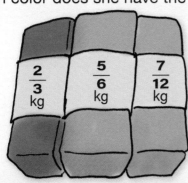

$\frac{2}{3}$ kg $\frac{5}{6}$ kg $\frac{7}{12}$ kg

$\frac{2}{3}$ $\frac{5}{6}$ $\frac{7}{12}$

☐   ☐   ☐

Practice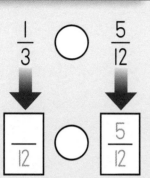

Use common denominators to compare the fractions.

$\dfrac{1}{3}$ ○ $\dfrac{5}{12}$

$\dfrac{}{12}$ ○ $\dfrac{5}{12}$

$\dfrac{6}{15}$ ○ $\dfrac{2}{5}$

$\dfrac{}{15}$ ○ $\dfrac{}{15}$

$\dfrac{3}{4}$ ○ $\dfrac{11}{16}$

☐ ○ ☐

Complete. Use common denominators.

Path	Length
Beach Path	$\dfrac{3}{5}$ km
Dune Path	$\dfrac{1}{2}$ km
Lookout Path	$\dfrac{7}{10}$ km

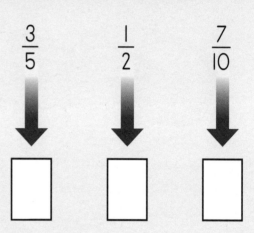

$\dfrac{3}{5}$ ☐ $\dfrac{1}{2}$ ☐ $\dfrac{7}{10}$ ☐

Which path is shortest?

Which path is longest?

Pet	Length
Gecko	$\dfrac{2}{3}$ ft.
Rabbit	$\dfrac{11}{12}$ ft.
Guinea Pig	$\dfrac{5}{6}$ ft.

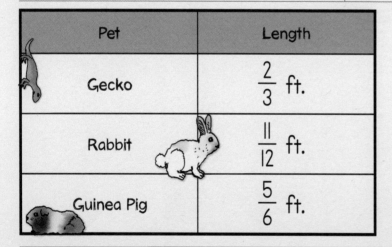
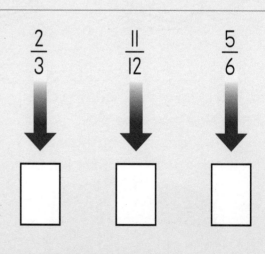

$\dfrac{2}{3}$ ☐ $\dfrac{11}{12}$ ☐ $\dfrac{5}{6}$ ☐

Which pet is shortest?

Which pet is longest?

Review

Circle the rhombuses. X the shapes that are not rhombuses.

Complete.

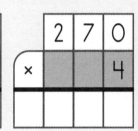

3	7	9
×		6

	2	7	0
×			4

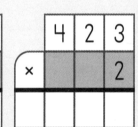

6	0	5
×		5

4	2	3
×		2

Circle the numbers that match the description. X the numbers that do not match the description.

Divisible by 2

36   792   891   4,678

Divisible by 5

71   700   772   4,785

Divisible by 10

30   450   910   3,290

Solve. Write the equations you use.

Liza has $8.00.
She buys a snack that costs $4.19.
How much money does she have left?

Holden has 5 feet of ribbon.
He uses 2 feet 7 inches to wrap a present.
How much ribbon does he have left?

Unit Wrap-Up 👤

Complete the equivalent fractions.

$$\frac{2}{3} = \frac{}{9}$$

$$\frac{1}{2} = \frac{4}{}$$

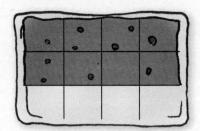

$$\frac{2}{3} = \frac{}{12}$$

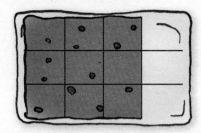

$$\frac{3}{4} = \frac{9}{}$$

Complete the equivalent fractions.

$$\frac{3}{4} = \frac{}{12}$$

$$\frac{1}{3} = \frac{5}{}$$

$$\frac{1}{2} = \frac{}{10}$$

$$\frac{3}{5} = \frac{}{10}$$

$$\frac{1}{4} = \frac{}{16}$$

$$\frac{2}{3} = \frac{}{9}$$

$$\frac{3}{10} = \frac{}{100}$$

$$\frac{7}{10} = \frac{70}{}$$

$$\frac{9}{10} = \frac{}{100}$$

Unit Wrap-Up

Use the printed rulers to measure the lines.

☐ in.

☐ in.

☐ in.

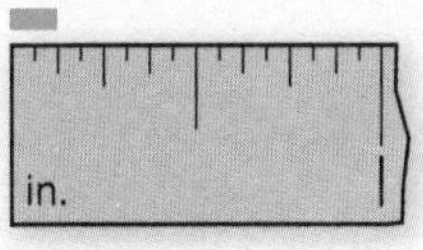

☐ in.

☐ in.

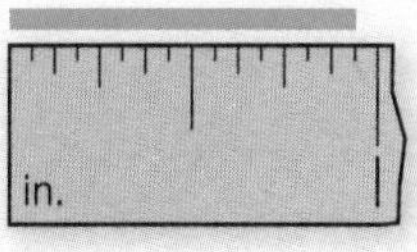

☐ in.

Use common denominators to compare the fractions.

$\frac{3}{4}$ ○ $\frac{7}{12}$

☐ ○ ☐

$\frac{7}{9}$ ○ $\frac{2}{3}$

☐ ○ ☐

$\frac{3}{8}$ ○ $\frac{5}{16}$

☐ ○ ☐

Solve. Use common denominators.

Bug	Length
Ant	$\frac{7}{16}$ in.
Pill Bug	$\frac{3}{8}$ in.
Ladybug	$\frac{1}{4}$ in.

$\frac{7}{16}$ → ☐

$\frac{3}{8}$ → ☐

$\frac{1}{4}$ → ☐

Which insect is shortest?

☐

Which insect is longest?

☐

Lesson Activities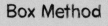

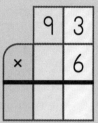

How much do 93 jars cost?

Box Method

Algorithm

$6

90   3

6

$6 \times 93 = $

$$\begin{array}{cc} 9 & 3 \\ \times & 6 \end{array}$$

How much do 78 jars cost?

$5

$5 \times 78 = $

$$\begin{array}{cc} 7 & 8 \\ \times & 5 \end{array}$$

B

How much do 325 loaves cost?

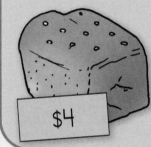

$4

300   20   5

4

$4 \times 325 = $

$$\begin{array}{ccc} 3 & 2 & 5 \\ \times & & 4 \end{array}$$

The sandwich shop sells 1,245 sandwiches.
Each sandwich costs $7.
How much money does the shop earn?

$7 \times 1,245 = $

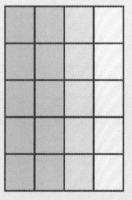

$$\begin{array}{cccc} 1, & 2 & 4 & 5 \\ \times & & & 7 \end{array}$$

Practice   Complete.

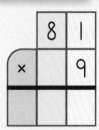

	8	1
×		9

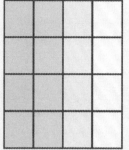

80   1

9 [|]

81 × 9 = [   ]

	2	4	9
×			5

[| |]

249 × 5 = [   ]

	1,	9	6	2
×				4

[| | |]

1,962 × 4 = [   ]

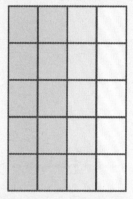

Use the box method or multiplication algorithm to solve.

The playroom is 13 m long and 7 m wide. What is its area?

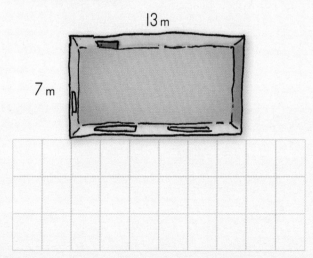

13 m

7 m

The banner is 27 cm long and 6 cm wide. What is its area?

27 cm

6 cm   congratulations!

Review 👤 Write whether each triangle is acute, right, or obtuse.

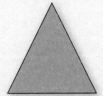

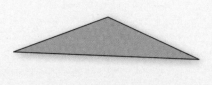

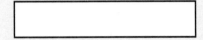
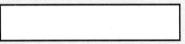
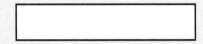

Complete the missing fractions on the number lines.

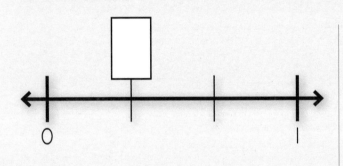
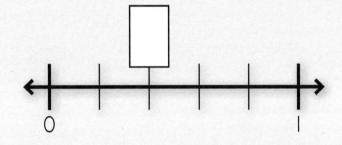

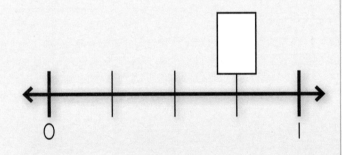

Solve. Write the equations you use.

I have 4 feet of string.
If I cut the string into 6 equal pieces,
how many inches long will each piece be?

Preston jumps 35 inches.
Prema jumps 17 inches farther than Preston.
How far does Prema jump in feet and inches?

Lesson 13.1

Lesson Activities 👥

Area Model

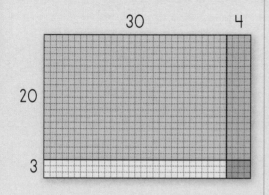

Box Method

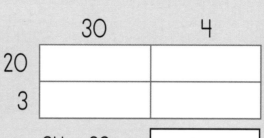

$$34 \times 23 = \boxed{}$$

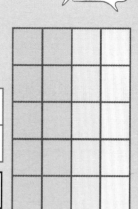

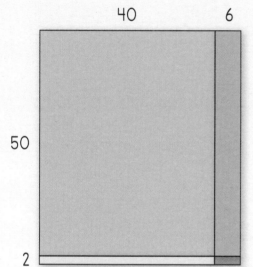

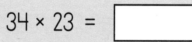

$$46 \times 52 = \boxed{}$$

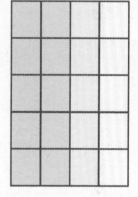

The Product Game

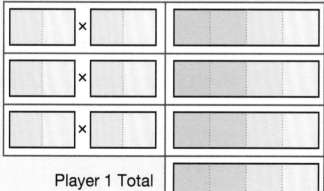

Player 1 Total

Player 2 Total

Practice

Complete the boxes to find the products.

	10	6
30		
4		

16 × 34 = [ ]

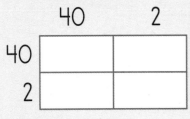

	20	9
30		
5		

29 × 35 = [ ]

	40	2
40		
2		

42 × 42 = [ ]

	60	2
30		
7		

62 × 37 = [ ]

	70	9
20		
1		

79 × 21 = [ ]

	80	6
40		
3		

86 × 43 = [ ]

Complete the boxes to find the area.

The soccer field is 45 yards long and 35 yards wide.
What is its area?

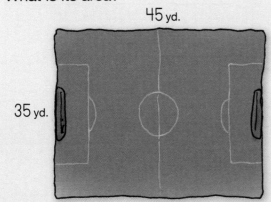

45 yd.

35 yd.

	40	5
30		
5		

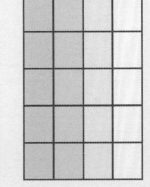

45 × 35 = [ ] sq. yd.

Review — Write each number in the place-value chart.

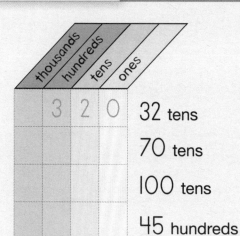

thousands	hundreds	tens	ones
3	2	0	

32 tens

70 tens

100 tens

45 hundreds

99 hundreds

Complete.

[ ] + 75 = 100

[ ] + 35 = 100

[ ] + 45 = 100

[ ] + 89 = 100

[ ] + 64 = 100

Draw a line to match each measurement. Then, complete the conversion.

5 cm 3 mm = [ ] mm

40 mm = [ ] cm

6 cm = [ ] mm

37 mm = [ ] cm [ ] mm

Solve. Write the equations you use.

Each pack of gum has 8 sticks.

- How many sticks of gum are in 30 packs?

- How many sticks of gum are in 4 packs?

- How many sticks of gum are in 34 packs?

13.3

Lesson Activities 👥

You earn 3 ten-dollar bills each time you referee a soccer game.

A

14 games	18 games	21 games

```
   1 4          1 8          2 1
 ×   3        ×   3        ×   3
```

B

You earn $30 each time you referee a soccer game.
How much do you earn if you referee 26 games?

```
   2 6
 × 3 0
```

C

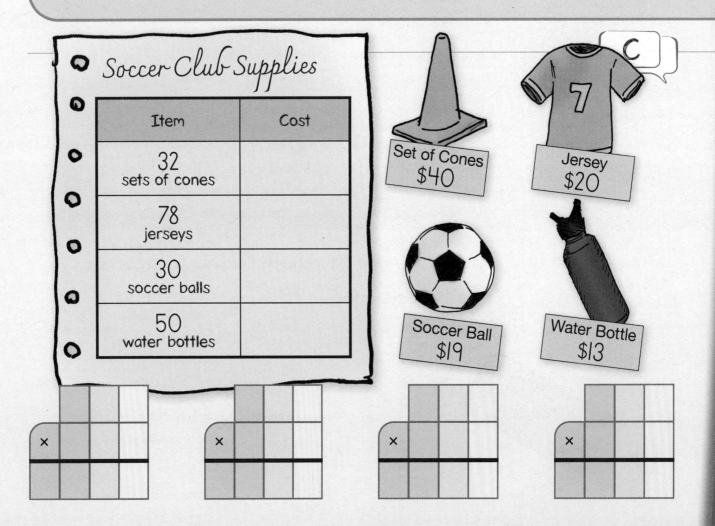

Soccer Club Supplies

Item	Cost
32 sets of cones	
78 jerseys	
30 soccer balls	
50 water bottles	

Set of Cones $40

Jersey $20

Soccer Ball $19

Water Bottle $13

Practice 👤 Complete. Use the example to help.

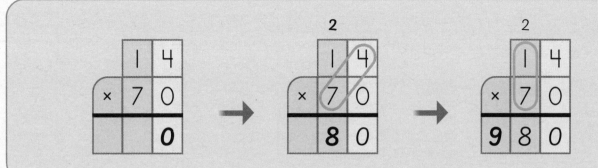

	8	3
×	2	0

	6	7
×	3	0

	9	4
×	5	0

	6	3
×	6	0

Solve. Write the equations you use.

The swimming pool is 30 yards long.
There are 36 inches in a yard.
How many inches long is the pool?

Noa earns $35 per hour.
She works 40 hours per week.
How much does she earn each week?

A professional basketball court is 94 ft. long and 50 ft. wide. What is its area?

⭐ There are 60 minutes in one hour. How many minutes are in one day?

Review 👤 Complete the equivalent fractions.

$$\frac{2}{3} = \frac{\boxed{}}{21}$$

$$\frac{5}{6} = \frac{25}{\boxed{}}$$

$$\frac{7}{10} = \frac{\boxed{}}{40}$$

$$\frac{1}{5} = \frac{\boxed{}}{10}$$

$$\frac{3}{8} = \frac{6}{\boxed{}}$$

$$\frac{1}{2} = \frac{20}{\boxed{}}$$

Complete.

$90 \div 3 = \boxed{}$

$100 \div 2 = \boxed{}$

$200 \div 5 = \boxed{}$

$280 \div 4 = \boxed{}$

$160 \div 2 = \boxed{}$

Complete.

$7 \text{ cm} = \boxed{} \text{ mm}$

$4 \text{ m} = \boxed{} \text{ cm}$

$90 \text{ mm} = \boxed{} \text{ cm}$

$800 \text{ cm} = \boxed{} \text{ m}$

$6 \text{ ft.} = \boxed{} \text{ in.}$

$8 \text{ yd.} = \boxed{} \text{ ft.}$

$48 \text{ in.} = \boxed{} \text{ ft.}$

$33 \text{ ft.} = \boxed{} \text{ yd.}$

Match.

| line segment | ray | point | line |

Lesson Activities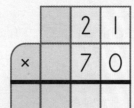

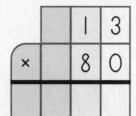
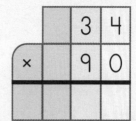

	2	1
×	7	0

	1	3
×	8	0

	3	4
×	9	0

$24

How much do 6 sets cost?

		2	4
×			6

How much do 20 sets cost?

		2	4
×		2	0

How much do 24 sets cost?

		2	4
×		2	6

$15

7 sketchbooks

		1	5
×			7

30 sketchbooks

		1	5
×		3	0

37 sketchbooks

		1	5
×		3	7

$18

4 blocks of clay

		1	8
×			4

30 blocks of clay

		1	8
×		3	0

34 blocks of clay

		1	8
×		3	4

Practice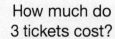

Complete the problems to answer the questions.

Trampoline park tickets cost $16 per person.

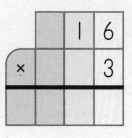

How much do 3 tickets cost?

	1	6
×		3

How much do 20 tickets cost?

	1	6
×	2	0

How much do 23 tickets cost?

	1	6
×	2	3

There are 75 paper clips in each box.

How many paper clips are in 9 boxes?

	7	5
×		9

How many paper clips are in 30 boxes?

	7	5
×	3	0

How many paper clips are in 39 boxes?

	7	5
×	3	9

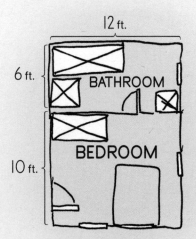

12 ft.

6 ft.

BATHROOM

10 ft.

BEDROOM

What is the area of the bathroom?

	1	2
×		6

What is the area of the bedroom?

	1	2
×	1	0

What is the area of both rooms?

	1	2
×	1	6

Lesson 13.4

Review

Draw a triangle to match each description.

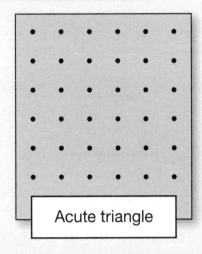

Acute triangle

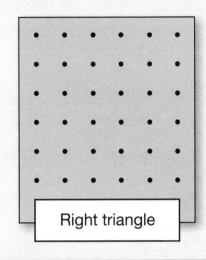

Right triangle

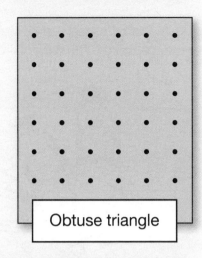

Obtuse triangle

Complete with <, >, or =.

25 in. ◯ 2 ft.

40 in. ◯ 4 ft.

72 in. ◯ 6 ft.

2 ft. ◯ 1 yd.

9 ft. ◯ 3 yd.

16 ft. ◯ 5 yd.

5,280 ft. ◯ 1 mi.

10,000 ft. ◯ 2 mi.

20,000 ft. ◯ 3 mi.

Find the length of each missing side.

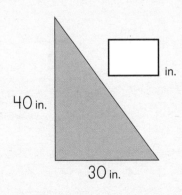

40 in.

30 in.

Perimeter: 120 in.

All sides are equal.

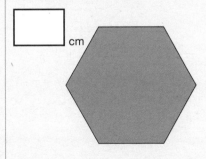

cm

Perimeter: 120 cm

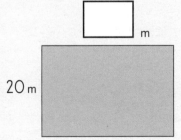

m

20 m

⭐ Area: 600 sq. m

13.5

Lesson Activities 👥

Each set of oil paints costs $21. How much do 35 sets cost?

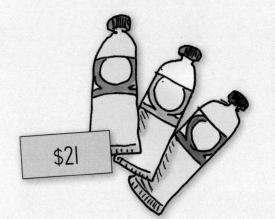

$21

How much do 5 sets cost?

```
    2  1
×      5
─────────
```

How much do 30 sets cost?

```
    2  1
×   3  0
─────────
```

How much do 35 sets cost?

```
    2  1
×   3  5
─────────
```

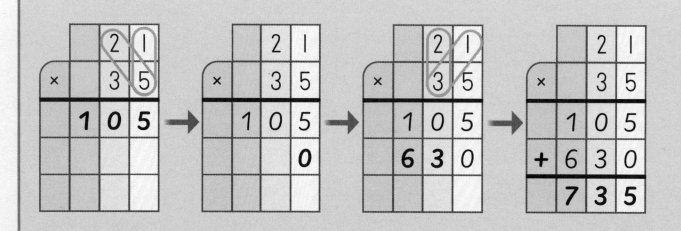

```
    2̸  1̸
×   3  5
─────────
1  0  5
```
→
```
    2  1
×   3  5
─────────
1  0  5
         0
```
→
```
    2̸  1̸
×   3  5
─────────
1  0  5
6  3  0
```
→
```
    2  1
×   3  5
─────────
   1  0  5
+  6  3  0
─────────
   7  3  5
```

```
    3  2
×   5  4
─────────
```

```
    2  5
×   6  4
─────────
```

```
    2  3
×   7  4
─────────
```

The Product Game

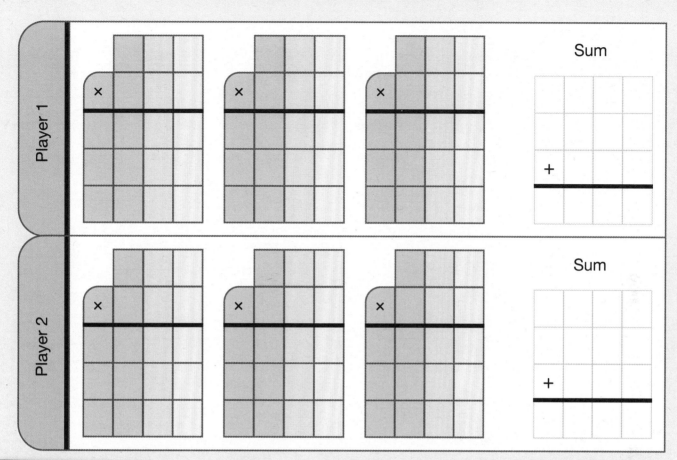

					Sum
Player 1	×	×	×	+
Player 2	×	×	×	+

Practice

Multiply to solve the word problems.

Each box has 45 erasers.
How many erasers are in 16 boxes?

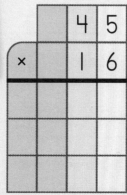

```
      4 5
  ×   1 6
  ─────────
```

Each pack has 36 sheets of
origami paper.
How many sheets are in 25 packs?

```
      3 6
  ×   2 5
  ─────────
```

Review 👤 Use common denominators to compare the fractions.

$$\frac{5}{9} \bigcirc \frac{2}{3}$$

$$\boxed{\frac{5}{9}} \bigcirc \boxed{\frac{}{9}}$$

$$\frac{1}{4} \bigcirc \frac{3}{12}$$

$$\square \bigcirc \square$$

$$\frac{6}{10} \bigcirc \frac{65}{100}$$

$$\square \bigcirc \square$$

Use the diagram to tell whether each statement is true or false.

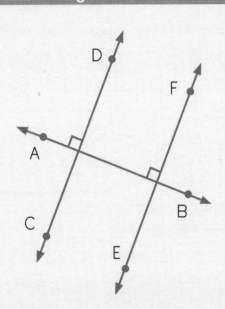

$\overleftrightarrow{AB} \parallel \overleftrightarrow{CD}$	$\overleftrightarrow{AB} \perp \overleftrightarrow{CD}$
T **F**	**T** **F**
$\overleftrightarrow{AB} \parallel \overleftrightarrow{EF}$	$\overleftrightarrow{AB} \perp \overleftrightarrow{EF}$
T **F**	**T** **F**
$\overleftrightarrow{CD} \parallel \overleftrightarrow{EF}$	$\overleftrightarrow{CD} \perp \overleftrightarrow{EF}$
T **F**	**T** **F**

Use the clues to complete the chart.

- The bulldog weighs 40 pounds.

- The bulldog weighs 8 times more than the chihuahua.

- The bulldog weighs half as much as the German shepherd.

- The bulldog weighs 25 pounds less than the golden retriever.

Dog	Weight (pounds)
Bulldog	
Chihuahua	
German Shepherd	
Golden Retriever	

Lesson Activities 👥

A

Estimate

```
    4 6
×   3 3
```

× _____

B

Snowball Fight

37 93 28 54 58 61 64 75 82 44

Player 1

×   ×   ×

Sum

+

Player 2

×   ×   ×

Sum

+

13.6

Practice 👤   **Estimate the product for each problem. Then, find the exact answer. Use the sample problem to help.**

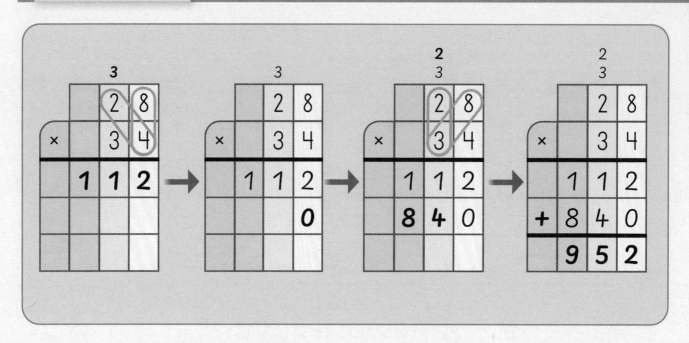

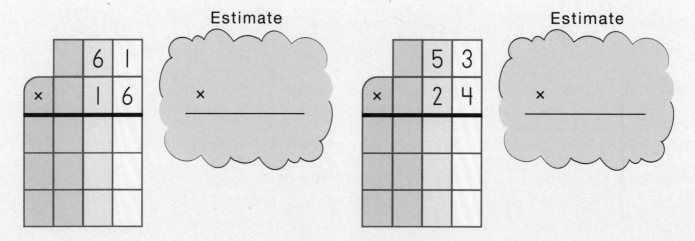

Estimate

× _____

Estimate

× _____

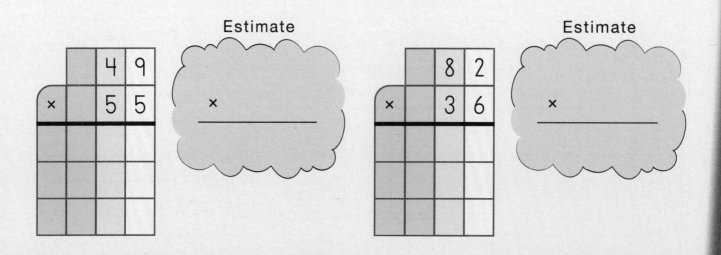

Estimate

× _____

Estimate

× _____

Review 👤 Complete the missing fractions on the number lines.

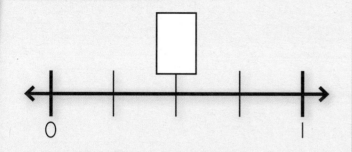

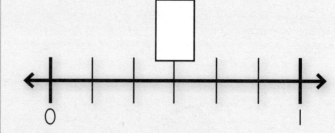

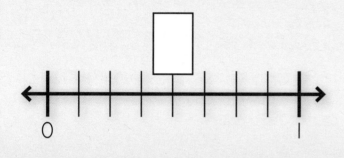

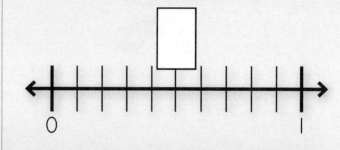

Use the words in the word bank to label the shapes.
Use the most specific name possible.

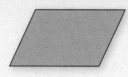

| trapezoid |
| parallelogram |
| rectangle |
| square |
| rhombus |

Complete.

	5 cm	8 mm
+	3 cm	2 mm
↺		

	4 m	8 cm
+	1 m	60 cm
↺		

	2 km	600 m
+	3 km	600 m
↺		

Lesson Activities

Maggie earns $13 per hour as a babysitter.
In May, she works 18 hours.
How much money does she earn?

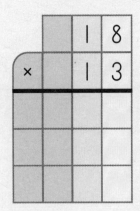

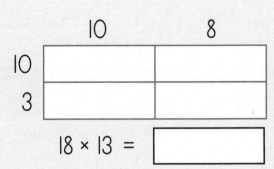

$18 \times 13 =$ ____

Would you rather work 28 hours and get paid $17 per hour...

...or would you rather work 22 hours and get paid $19 per hour?

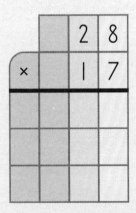

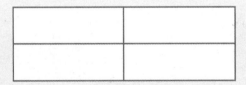

$22 \times 19 =$ ____

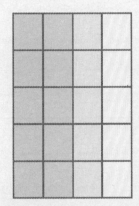

Would you rather pay $35 per lesson for 16 tap dance lessons...

...or would you rather pay $42 per lesson for 12 tap dance lessons?

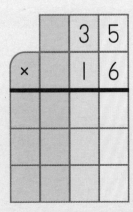

$42 \times 12 =$ ____

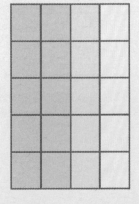

Practice 👤 Solve. You may use the multiplication algorithm or box method.

Each box of crackers has 37 crackers.
How many crackers are in 15 boxes?

36 inches equal 1 yard.
How many inches equal 15 yards?

Find the missing digits.

```
      7 1
    ×   4 2
      1 □ 2
  + 2 □ 4 □
  □ □ □ □
```

⭐
```
      2 3
    ×   □ □
      1 6 1
  + 1 3 8 0
    1,5 4 1
```

⭐
```
      □ 4
    ×   □ 3
      1 9 □
  + 2 5 6 0
    2,7 5 □
```

Find the missing numbers.

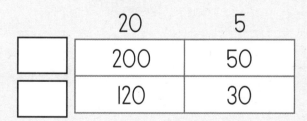

	20	5
□	200	50
□	120	30

⭐
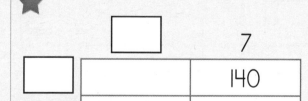

	□	7
		140
4	120	

25 × [ ] = 400

[ ] × [ ] = 888

Review   Complete the equivalent fractions.

$\dfrac{1}{2} = \dfrac{\boxed{}}{10}$ $\dfrac{1}{5} = \dfrac{\boxed{}}{10}$ $\dfrac{3}{5} = \dfrac{\boxed{}}{10}$

$\dfrac{4}{10} = \dfrac{\boxed{}}{100}$ $\dfrac{8}{10} = \dfrac{\boxed{}}{100}$ $\dfrac{1}{10} = \dfrac{\boxed{}}{100}$

Match.

69 + 6	62	80 − 7
72 + 9	73	82 − 7
56 + 6	75	90 − 9
65 + 8	81	89 − 6
78 + 5	83	71 − 9

Use the printed rulers to measure the lines.   Complete.

 $\dfrac{\boxed{}}{10}$ cm $\dfrac{\boxed{}}{10}$ cm

 $\dfrac{\boxed{}}{10}$ cm $\dfrac{\boxed{}}{10}$ cm

11:45 p.m.  min. → 12:15 a.m.

11:55 p.m.  min. → 12:30 a.m.

11:40 p.m.  min. → 12:25 a.m.

Unit Wrap-Up 👤

Complete.

	3	8
×	6	2

	20	3
80		
7		

23 × 87 = ☐

Describe the mistake in each problem. Then, solve it correctly.

incorrect ✗

		2	
		4	7
×		3	1
		4	7
+	1	4	1
	1	8	8

What is the mistake?

Correct solution:

		4	7
×		3	1

---

incorrect ✗

	20	9
60	1,200	560
7	140	63

29 × 67 = ☐ 1,963

	1	2	0	0
		5	6	0
		1	4	0
+			6	3
	1	9	6	3

What is the mistake?

Correct solution:

	20	9
60		
7		

29 × 67 = ☐

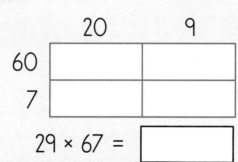

Unit Wrap-Up 👤

Kids' Club End-of-Year Field Trip Options

Vote for one option:

○ **Water Park**
$43 per ticket

○ **Theme Park**
$86 per ticket

○ **Zoo**
$19 per ticket

○ **Laser Tag**
$27 per ticket

How much do 35 tickets to the water park cost?

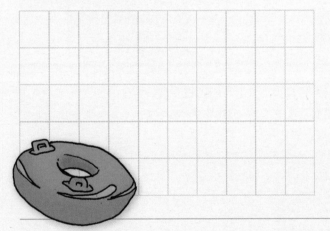

How much do 35 tickets to the zoo cost?

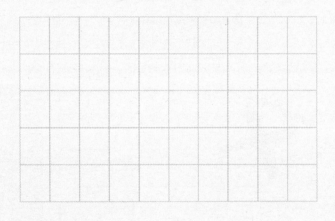

How much do 35 laser tag tickets cost?

How much do 35 tickets to the theme park cost?

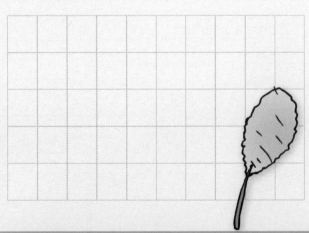

Lesson Activities 👥

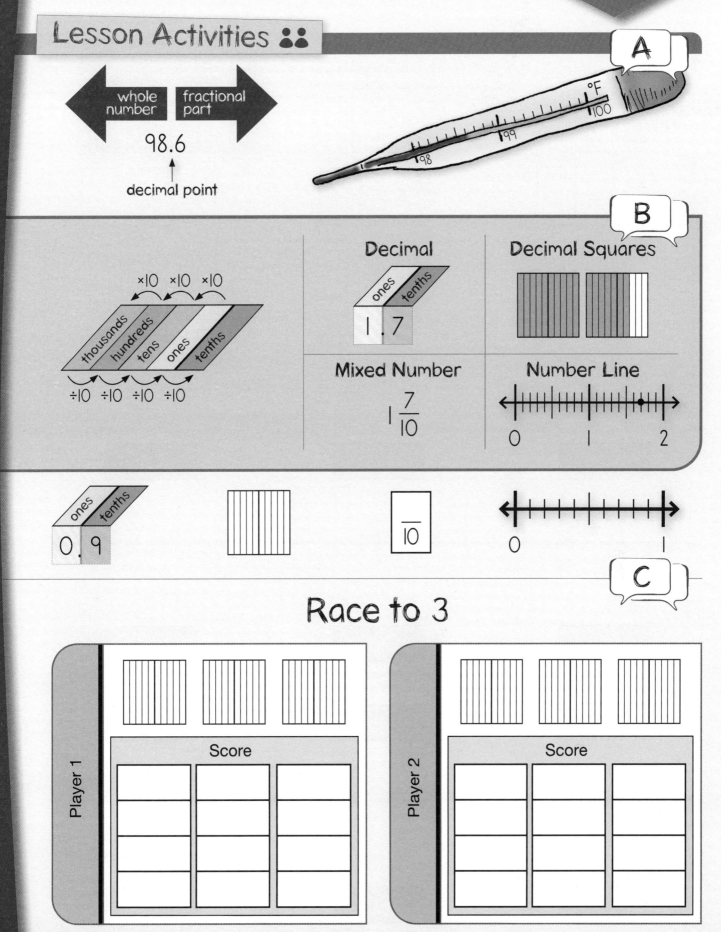

A

whole number ← → fractional part

98.6

↑ decimal point

°F 100 99 98

B

thousands hundreds tens ones tenths

×10 ×10 ×10

÷10 ÷10 ÷10 ÷10

Decimal

ones tenths

1.7

Decimal Squares

Mixed Number

1 7/10

Number Line

0   1   2

ones tenths

0.9

$\overline{10}$

0   1

C

Race to 3

Player 1

Score

Player 2

Score

Practice

Color the decimal squares to match.
Then, write a fraction or mixed number to match.

 0.1 = $\dfrac{}{10}$

 0.5 = ☐

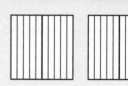 1.3 = ☐

 0.4 = ☐

 0.9 = ☐

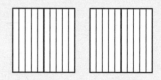 1.8 = ☐

Connect each number to its place on the number line.

| 0.5 | 0.1 | 1.3 |

0   1   2

| 0.4 | 1.8 | 0.9 |

Connect each number to its dot on the number line.

| 1.5 | 0.2 | 3.9 |

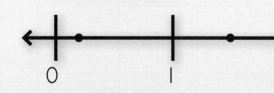

0   1   2   3   4   5

| 2.7 | 3.1 | 4.6 |

Lesson 14.1

Review

Write a fraction to complete each equation. Convert the fraction to a whole number or mixed number if possible.

$\frac{21}{10} - \frac{8}{10}$ = ☐ = ☐

$\frac{6}{10} + \frac{5}{10}$ = ☐ = ☐

$5 \times \frac{4}{10}$ = ☐ = ☐

$3 \times \frac{6}{10}$ = ☐ = ☐

Complete.

	3	8
×	4	5

	6	1
×	4	8

Complete with <, >, or =.

13,974 ◯ 13,947

13,008 ◯ 13,080

2,461 ◯ 20,461

17,685 ◯ 17,685

Write each length as a fraction or mixed number.

8 mm = ☐/10 cm

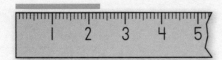

2 cm 3 mm = ☐ cm

Complete.

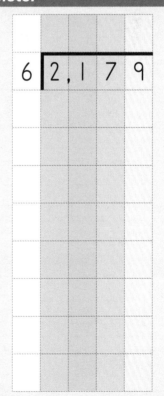

6) 2,1 7 9

Lesson Activities 👥

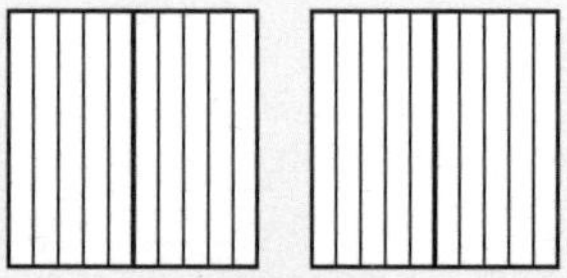

1.8 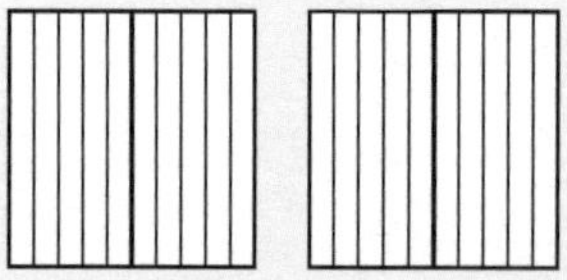   1.2 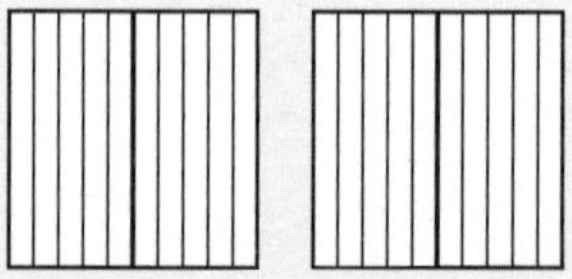   0.9

1.8 ◯ 1.2	1.2 ◯ 0.9	1.8 ◯ 2
0.3 ◯ 3	2 ◯ 2.0	2.5 ◯ 1.9

Decimal Least to Greatest

2	0.2	3	2	4	1.4
5	0.9	6	0.6	7	1	8	1.8
9	1.3	10	0.7	11	0	12	1.9

Player 1

least   greatest

Player 2

least   greatest

Practice

**Color the decimal squares to match.
Then, complete the circles with <, >, or =.**

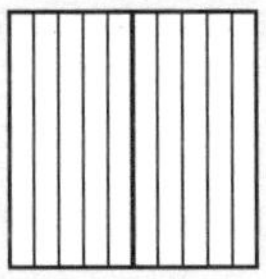

0.6 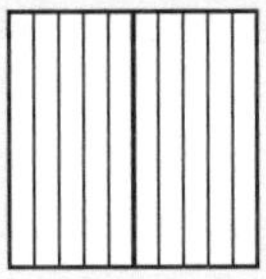　　　　　0.4 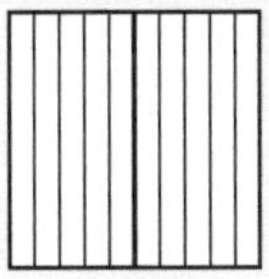　　　　　0.9

0.6 ◯ 0.4

0.4 ◯ 0.9

0.6 ◯ 0.9

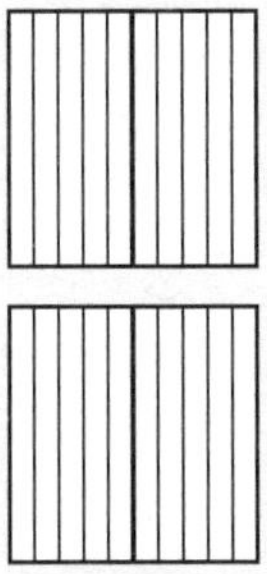

1.2 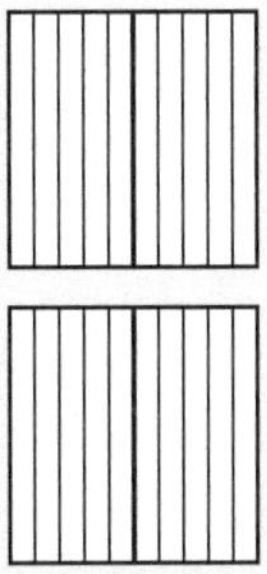　　　　　0.2 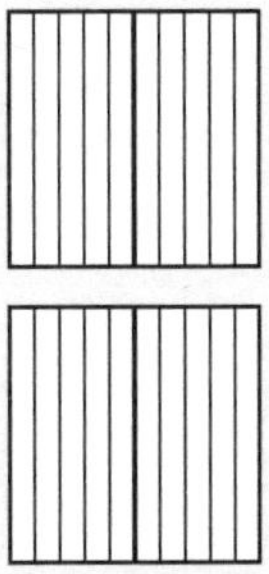　　　　　2.0

1.2 ◯ 0.2

0.2 ◯ 2.0

1.2 ◯ 2.0

Complete the circles with <, >, or =.

0.7 ◯ 0.5　　　　　1.2 ◯ 1.4　　　　　2.1 ◯ 1.8

0.9 ◯ 1　　　　　3 ◯ 3.0　　　　　4.9 ◯ 5

Write the numbers in order from least to greatest.

0.6　　　0.5

0.1　　　0.8

least			greatest

0.7　　　1.4

2　　　1

least			greatest

Review 👤 Complete the chart.

Standard Form	Expanded Form
18,401	
	100,000 + 8,000 + 400 + 10
	100,000 + 80,000 + 40 + 1

Complete.

| 2 | 7 | 2 | 7 | | 5 | 9 | 3 | 5 | | 7 | 3 | 2 | 0 |

Complete with <, >, or =.

$\frac{1}{2}$ ◯ $\frac{9}{10}$

$\frac{1}{2}$ ◯ $\frac{1}{10}$

$\frac{9}{10}$ ◯ $\frac{7}{10}$

$3\frac{1}{10}$ ◯ $2\frac{4}{10}$

Solve. Write your equations in the work space.

The vegetable garden is 24 feet long and 18 feet wide.

- What is the perimeter of the vegetable garden?

- What is the area of the vegetable garden?

WORK SPACE

Lesson Activities

Decimal

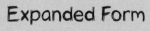

$$÷10 \quad ÷10$$

Decimal Squares

Mixed Number	Expanded Form
$1\frac{65}{100}$	$1 + \frac{6}{10} + \frac{5}{100}$

Decimal	Decimal Squares	Fraction or Mixed Number	Expanded Form
0.49			
1.37			
0.25			
0.07			

B

Practice

Color the decimal squares to match.
Then, write a fraction or a mixed number to match.

$0.51 = \dfrac{}{100}$

$0.62 = \boxed{}$

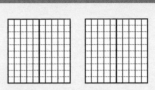

$1.15 = \boxed{}$

$0.09 = \boxed{}$

$0.9 = \boxed{}$

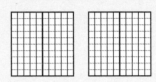

$1.99 = \boxed{}$

Complete the chart.

Decimal	Mixed Number	Expanded Form
6.25		
	$4\dfrac{31}{100}$	
7.80		
		$5 + \dfrac{7}{100}$

Complete the sequences.

0.7   0.8   0.9   _   _   _   _   1.4

1.95   1.96   1.97   _   1.99   _   _   2.02

Review

Label the missing fractions on the number line.

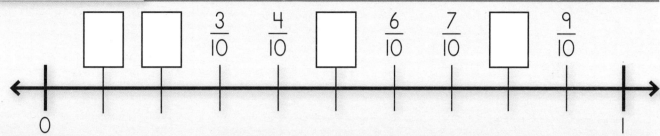

$\boxed{}$ $\boxed{}$ $\dfrac{3}{10}$ $\dfrac{4}{10}$ $\boxed{}$ $\dfrac{6}{10}$ $\dfrac{7}{10}$ $\boxed{}$ $\dfrac{9}{10}$

0   1

Use common denominators to compare the fractions.

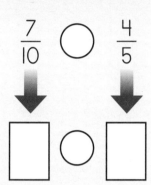

$\dfrac{7}{10}$ ◯ $\dfrac{4}{5}$

$\boxed{}$ ◯ $\boxed{}$

$\dfrac{1}{2}$ ◯ $\dfrac{6}{10}$

$\boxed{}$ ◯ $\boxed{}$

Complete the boxes to find the product.

	40	1
70		
8		

$41 \times 78 =$ $\boxed{}$

	90	9
20		
3		

$99 \times 23 =$ $\boxed{}$

Solve. Write your equations in the work space.

Kelsey practices the piano 45 minutes each day. How many minutes does she practice in 31 days?

One week, Karsen practices the trumpet 455 minutes. He practices the same amount each day. How many minutes does he practice each day?

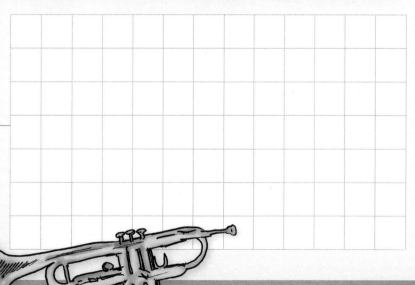

14.4

Lesson Activities 👥

1¢

$ [ ]

10¢

$ [ ]

$1 10¢ 10¢ 10¢ 1¢ 1¢ 1¢ 1¢

$ [ ]

0.54 ◯ 0.45

0.29 ◯ 0.3

0.40 ◯ 0.04

0.40 ◯ 0.4

Decimal War	2	0.52	3	0.8	4	0.49
5	0.06	6	0.35	7	0.28	8	0.4
9	0.42	10	0.7	11	0.6	12	0.64

Practice

Color the decimal squares to match.
Then, complete the circles with <, >, or =.

0.26   0.65   0.4

0.26 ◯ 0.65
0.65 ◯ 0.4
0.26 ◯ 0.4

0.8   0.08   0.80

0.8 ◯ 0.08
0.80 ◯ 0.08
0.8 ◯ 0.80

Complete the circles with <, >, or =.

2.37 ◯ 1.37   1.52 ◯ 1.68   6 ◯ 6.00

2.9 ◯ 2.09   2.9 ◯ 2.90   2.9 ◯ 2.99

Write the numbers in order from least to greatest.

1.48   1.08

1.04   1.4

☐ ☐ ☐ ☐
least   greatest

3   3.3

0.3   3.33

☐ ☐ ☐ ☐
least   greatest

14.4

Review Label the numbers on the number line.

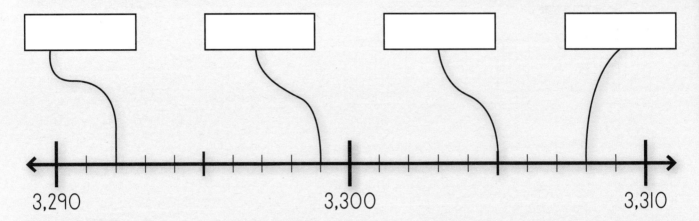

3,290   3,300   3,310

Complete the equivalent fractions.

$\frac{1}{3} = \frac{\boxed{}}{12}$ $\frac{5}{6} = \frac{15}{\boxed{}}$

$\frac{3}{4} = \frac{12}{\boxed{}}$ $\frac{3}{4} = \frac{\boxed{}}{20}$

$\frac{3}{10} = \frac{\boxed{}}{100}$ $\frac{6}{10} = \frac{60}{\boxed{}}$

Complete.

Solve. Write the equations you use.

Tyson buys a book for $6.89 and a bookmark for $1.38.
How much does he spend in all?

Miriam has $7.90.
She buys a pen for $3.37.
How much money does she have left?

Lesson Activities 👥

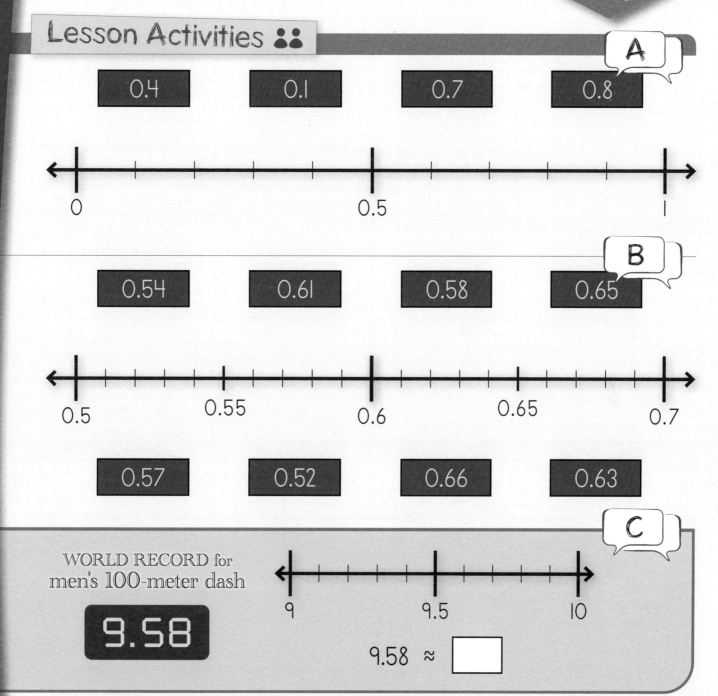

A

| 0.4 | 0.1 | 0.7 | 0.8 |

0   0.5   1

B

| 0.54 | 0.61 | 0.58 | 0.65 |

0.5   0.55   0.6   0.65   0.7

| 0.57 | 0.52 | 0.66 | 0.63 |

C

WORLD RECORD for
men's 100-meter dash

9.58

9   9.5   10

9.58 ≈ ☐

World Record	Exact Time (Seconds)	Time Rounded to Nearest Second
Women's 100-meter dash	10.49	
Men's 400-meter dash	43.03	
Women's 400-meter dash	47.60	

Practice

Label the numbers on the number line.

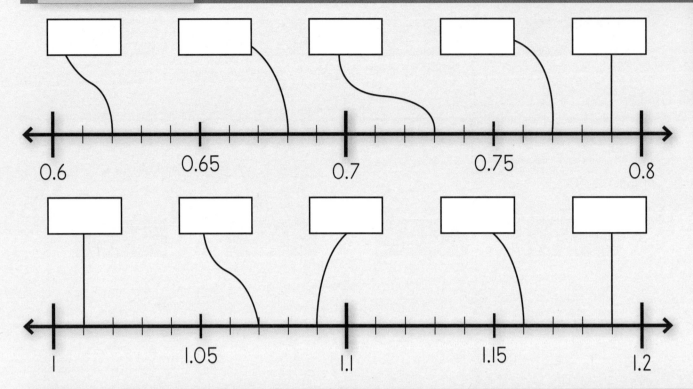

0.6   0.65   0.7   0.75   0.8

1   1.05   1.1   1.15   1.2

Choose the more sensible estimate for each dot on the number line.

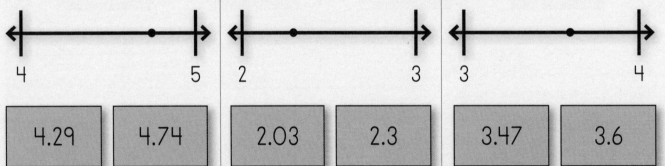

4   5   2   3   3   4

| 4.29 | 4.74 | 2.03 | 2.3 | 3.47 | 3.6 |

Round to the nearest whole number.

6.2 ≈ ☐   1.63 ≈ ☐   3.5 ≈ ☐

3.9 ≈ ☐   2.14 ≈ ☐   3.05 ≈ ☐

4.7 ≈ ☐   3.07 ≈ ☐   5.0 ≈ ☐

2.5 ≈ ☐   0.80 ≈ ☐   5.5 ≈ ☐

Review

Convert the mixed numbers to fractions.
Convert the fractions to mixed numbers or whole numbers.

$6\frac{5}{10} = \boxed{}$

$3\frac{2}{10} = \boxed{}$

$4\frac{9}{10} = \boxed{}$

$\frac{87}{10} = \boxed{}$

$\frac{17}{10} = \boxed{}$

$\frac{60}{10} = \boxed{}$

Complete.

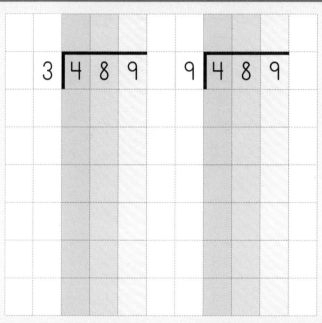

3 4 8 9   9 4 8 9

Complete.

1 ft. = $\boxed{}$ in.

1 yd. = $\boxed{}$ ft.

1 mi. = $\boxed{}$ ft.

1 cm = $\boxed{}$ mm

1 m = $\boxed{}$ cm

1 km = $\boxed{}$ m

Solve. Write the equations you use.

Nikki is 1 m 34 cm tall. Her little brother is 89 cm tall. How much taller is Nikki than her little brother?

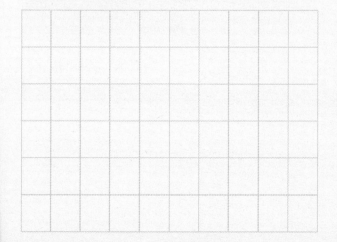

Mirabelle has 9 cm of wire. She cuts the wire into 5 equal pieces. How many millimeters long is each piece?

14.6

Lesson Activities 👥

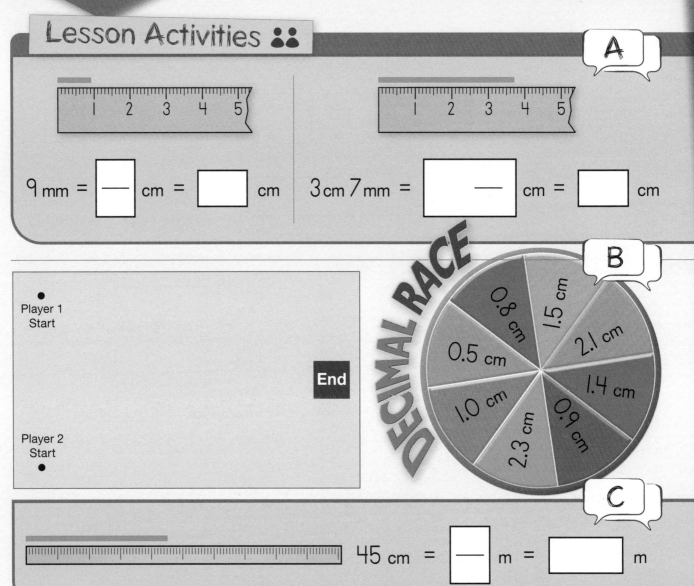

A

9 mm = [—] cm = [ ] cm

3 cm 7 mm = [—] cm = [ ] cm

B

DECIMAL RACE

Player 1 Start

Player 2 Start

End

Spinner: 0.8 cm, 1.5 cm, 2.1 cm, 1.4 cm, 0.9 cm, 2.3 cm, 1.0 cm, 0.5 cm

C

45 cm = [—] m = [ ] m

Men's Olympic Records

Event	High Jump	Pole Vault	Long Jump	Triple Jump
Record (m and cm)	2 m 39 cm	6 m 3 cm	8 m 90 cm	18 m 9 cm
Mixed Number (m)				
Decimal Number (m)				

Practice  **Write each length with a decimal point.**

2 cm 5 mm = ☐ cm

1 cm 4 mm = ☐ cm

4 cm 3 mm = ☐ cm

7 mm = ☐ cm

68 cm = ☐ m

35 cm = ☐ m

90 cm = ☐ m

6 cm = ☐ m

Complete the chart.

Women's Olympic Records

Event	High Jump	Pole Vault	Long Jump	Triple Jump
Record (m and cm)	2 m 6 cm	5 m 5 cm	7 m 40 cm	15 m 67 cm
Mixed Number (m)				
Decimal Number (m)				

Solve.

The ladybug is 0.3 cm long.
The ant is 0.41 cm long.
Which insect is shorter?

The purple ribbon is 0.84 m long.
The orange ribbon is 1.2 m long.
Which ribbon is longer?

Review 👤 Complete.

+	3 km	250 m
	1 km	150 m
↺		

-	6 cm	
	2 cm	3 mm

-	4 m	10 cm
	1 m	50 cm

Choose the more sensible measurement for each item.

Length of a paper clip

2.54 cm	2.54 mm

Length of a baseball bat

0.9 m	0.9 cm

Width of a license plate

0.3 cm	0.3 m

Solve. Write the equations you use.

The blue car costs $34,506.
The silver car costs $28,399.
How much more does the blue car cost than the silver car?

The rectangle's length is 3 times its width. What is the area of the rectangle?

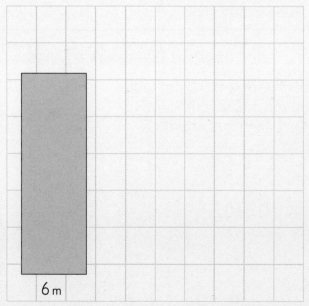

6 m

Lesson Activities 👥👥

A

kg

kg

kg

B

$\dfrac{1}{2} = \dfrac{}{10} = $ ▢

$\dfrac{1}{4} = \dfrac{}{100} = $ ▢

$\dfrac{3}{4} = \dfrac{}{100} = $ ▢

C

Victor needs at least $\frac{1}{2}$ lb. of tomatoes to make a salad. Which weights are more than $\frac{1}{2}$ lb.?

Heidi needs about $\frac{3}{4}$ kg of meat for a recipe. Which weight is closest to $\frac{3}{4}$ kg?

Cherry Tomatoes
Net weight:
0.53 lb.

Cherry Tomatoes
Net weight:
0.47 lb.

Cherry Tomatoes
Net weight:
0.39 lb.

Cherry Tomatoes
Net weight:
0.61 lb.

Fine Ground Meat
Net weight:
0.69 kg

Fine Ground Meat
Net weight:
0.78 kg

Fine Ground Meat
Net weight:
0.84 kg

Fine Ground Meat
Net weight:
0.7 kg

Practice

Complete each blank with a decimal.
You will use each decimal once.

0.25

0.5

0.75

$\frac{1}{2}$ = ☐ $\frac{3}{4}$ = ☐ $\frac{1}{4}$ = ☐

Complete the circles with <, >, or =.

0.43 ◯ $\frac{1}{2}$	0.52 ◯ $\frac{1}{2}$	0.5 ◯ $\frac{1}{2}$
0.25 ◯ $\frac{1}{4}$	0.28 ◯ $\frac{1}{4}$	0.21 ◯ $\frac{1}{4}$
0.92 ◯ $\frac{3}{4}$	0.68 ◯ $\frac{3}{4}$	0.75 ◯ $\frac{3}{4}$
1.82 ◯ $1\frac{3}{4}$	2.33 ◯ $2\frac{1}{2}$	4.25 ◯ $4\frac{1}{4}$

Follow the directions.

Ollie needs $\frac{1}{4}$ lb. of cheese for a recipe. Circle the packages with at least $\frac{1}{4}$ lb.

Alyssa needs about $\frac{1}{2}$ kg of clay to make a mug. Circle the package whose weight is closest to $\frac{1}{2}$ kg.

Cheddar Cheese
0.21 lb.

Cheddar Cheese
0.3 lb.

Cheddar Cheese
0.28 lb.

Cheddar Cheese
0.46 lb.

RED MODELING CLAY
0.6 kg

BLUE MODELING CLAY
0.49 kg

PURPLE MODELING CLAY
0.42 kg

GREEN MODELING CLAY
0.54 kg

Review 👤 Use both methods to find the product.

	8	2
×	3	4

	80	2
30		
4		

82 × 34 = ⬚

Find the missing angle measure. | Complete.

⬚

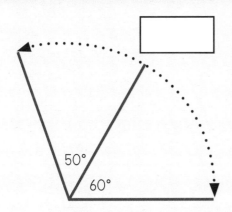

50°

60°

	3 ft.	8 in.
+	2 ft.	9 in.

	6 ft.	2 in.
-	3 ft.	5 in.

Solve. Write the equations you use.

Toni has $6\frac{3}{10}$ kg of apples. She uses $2\frac{7}{10}$ kg to make applesauce. How many kilograms of apples does she have left?

Andrew's bedroom is 9 feet wide. It has an area of 162 square feet. What is his bedroom's length?

Unit Wrap-Up

Color the decimal and write a fraction to match.

$0.8 = \boxed{}$

$0.08 = \boxed{}$

$0.88 = \boxed{}$

Complete the chart.

Decimal	Mixed Number	Expanded Form
1.36		
	$4\frac{6}{100}$	
		$3 + \frac{5}{10} + \frac{8}{100}$

Label the numbers on the number line.

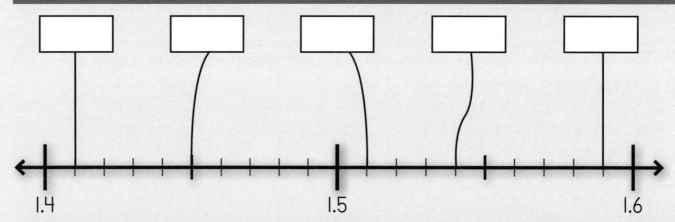

Complete the circles with <, >, or =.

0.7 ◯ 0.53   2.73 ◯ 3.1

0.9 ◯ 1   4.3 ◯ 4.09

0.5 ◯ 0.4   2 ◯ 2.0

Round to the nearest whole number.

$3.8 \approx \boxed{}$

$4.29 \approx \boxed{}$

$6.01 \approx \boxed{}$

Unit Wrap-Up 👤

Complete the chart. Include the correct units.

Length	Mixed Number	Decimal
4 cm 1 mm		
	$2\frac{3}{10}$ cm	
		1.6 cm
1 m 24 cm		
	$4\frac{5}{100}$ m	
		2.96 m

Write each measurement as a decimal.

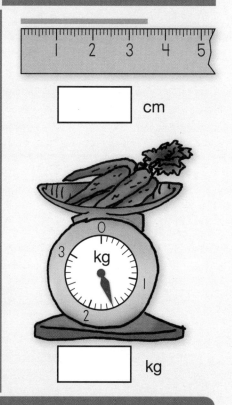

[ ] cm

[ ] kg

Answer the questions.

Griffin has 0.78 kg of orange modeling clay, 1.04 kg of purple modeling clay, and 1.2 kg of yellow modeling clay.

- Which color does he have the most of?

- Which color does he have the least of?

| 0.78 kg | 1.04 kg | 1.2 kg |

Maya completes the obstacle course in 12.05 seconds. Shivon completes the obstacle course in 12.73 seconds. Who has the shorter time?

Ari needs at least $\frac{1}{2}$ kg of blueberries to make muffins. Which packages have more than $\frac{1}{2}$ kg? Circle them.

Organic Blueberries
Net weight: 0.42 kg

Organic Blueberries
Net weight: 0.63 kg

Organic Blueberries
Net weight: 0.54 kg

Lesson Activities 👥

Minutes	Seconds
1	
2	
3	
4	
5	

Hours	Minutes
1	
2	
3	
4	
5	

Days	Hours
1	
2	
3	
4	
5	

B

3 min. 1 sec. = ⬚ sec.

4 hr. 15 min. = ⬚ min.

2 days 3 hr. = ⬚ hr.

125 sec. = ⬚ min. ⬚ sec.

200 min. = ⬚ hr. ⬚ min.

98 hr. = ⬚ days ⬚ hr.

C

Time Three in a Row

Player 1 START →	315 sec.	5 days 1 hr.	195 min.	1 hr. 30 min.	49 hr.
5 hr. 25 min.	2 min. 15 sec.	90 min.	265 sec.	2 days 1 hr.	2 min. 45 sec.
295 min.	4 min. 10 sec.	1 hr. 15 min.	5 min. 15 sec.	140 min.	135 sec.
1 day 10 hr.	121 hr.	4 hr. 55 min.	80 hr.	34 hr.	3 days 8 hr.
250 sec.	3 days 3 hr.	3 hr. 15 min.	325 min.	165 sec.	Player 2 START ←
	4 min. 25 sec.	75 hr.	2 hr. 20 min.	75 min.	

Practice 👤 Complete with <, >, or =.

50 sec. ◯ 1 min.   185 sec. ◯ 3 min.   240 sec. ◯ 6 min.

100 min. ◯ 1 hr.   119 min. ◯ 2 hr.   300 min. ◯ 5 hr.

25 hr. ◯ 1 day   40 hr. ◯ 2 days   50 hr. ◯ 2 days

Complete.

7 min. = [   ] sec.   120 sec. = [   ] min.

7 min. 30 sec. = [   ] sec.   129 sec. = [   ] min. [   ] sec.

5 hr. = [   ] min.   240 min. = [   ] hr.

5 hr. 2 min. = [   ] min.   241 min. = [   ] hr. [   ] min.

2 days = [   ] hr.   24 hr. = [   ] days

2 days 5 hr. = [   ] hr.   36 hr. = [   ] days [   ] hr.

Solve.

The world record for standing on one foot with your eyes closed is about 1 hr. 8 min. How many minutes is that?

The world record for standing on one foot with your eyes open is about 3 days and 5 hours. How many hours is that?

Review 👤 Complete.

+	6 ft.	10 in.
	2 ft.	3 in.
↻		

+	2 m	50 cm
	3 m	50 cm
↻		

+	1 km	400 m
	2 km	50 m
↻		

−	5 ft.	7 in.
	4 ft.	3 in.

−	4 m	
	1 m	85 cm

−	3 km	200 m
	1 km	600 m

Complete the circles with <, >, or =.

2.3 ◯ 3.2

9.0 ◯ 0.9

0.83 ◯ 0.38

0.50 ◯ 0.05

4.72 ◯ 4.27

Complete.

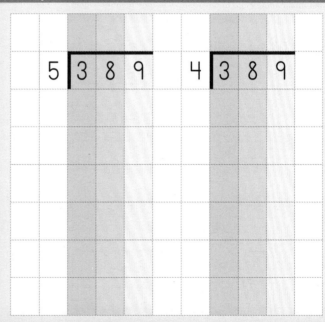

5 | 3 | 8 | 9   4 | 3 | 8 | 9

Solve. Write the equations you use.

Rainy Day Special

Umbrellas $12   Ponchos $8

Dylan's family buys 3 umbrellas and 5 ponchos. How much do they spend?

Lesson Activities 👥

	3 hr.	15 min.
+	2 hr.	30 min.
↻		

	1 min.	40 sec.
+	2 min.	30 sec.
↻		

	5 hr.	
−	2 hr.	40 min.

	6 min.	15 sec.
−	2 min.	35 sec.

Race to 10 Hours

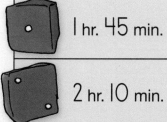 1 hr. 45 min.

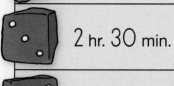 2 hr. 10 min.

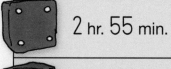 2 hr. 30 min.

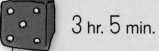 2 hr. 55 min.

3 hr. 5 min.

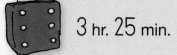 3 hr. 25 min.

	Player 1			Player 2	
	hr.	min.		hr.	min.
+	hr.	min.	+	hr.	min.
↻	hr.	min.	↻	hr.	min.
	hr.	min.		hr.	min.
+	hr.	min.	+	hr.	min.
↻	hr.	min.	↻	hr.	min.
	hr.	min.		hr.	min.
+	hr.	min.	+	hr.	min.
↻	hr.	min.	↻	hr.	min.
	hr.	min.		hr.	min.
+	hr.	min.	+	hr.	min.

Practice 👤 Complete.

	hr.	min.
+	3 hr.	30 min.
	2 hr.	20 min.

	hr.	min.
+	1 hr.	15 min.
	2 hr.	45 min.

	min.	sec.
+	5 min.	40 sec.
	1 min	30 sec.

	2 hr.	30 min.
−	1 hr.	10 min.

	4 hr.	
−	1 hr.	50 min.

	6 min.	5 sec.
−	3 min.	30 sec.

Charlotte made a chart of how much time she spent babysitting. Use the chart to answer the questions.

Monday: 2 hr. 20 min.

Tuesday: 3 hr. 10 min.

Saturday: 1 hr. 45 min.

How much time did she spend babysitting on Monday and Tuesday?

How much more time did she spend babysitting on Tuesday than Monday?

How much time did she spend babysitting in all?

Review

Choose the more reasonable estimate for each angle.

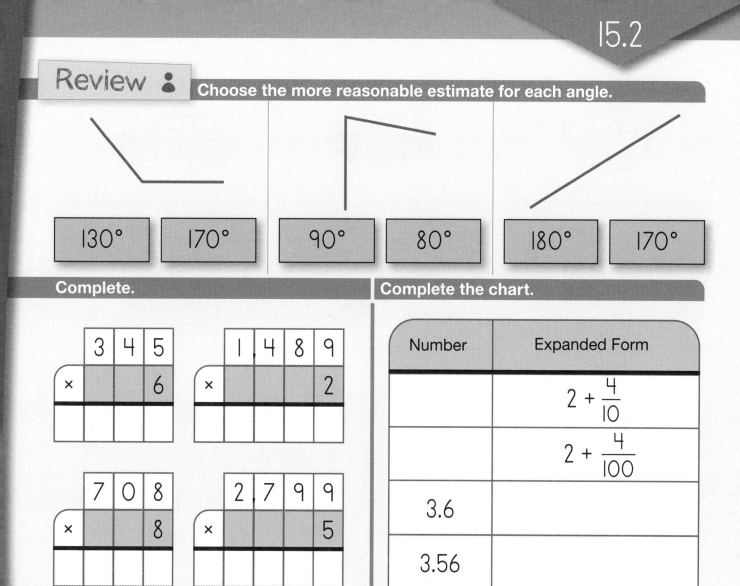

| 130° | 170° | | 90° | 80° | | 180° | 170° |

Complete.

```
  3 4 5
×     6
```

```
  1,4 8 9
×       2
```

```
  7 0 8
×     8
```

```
  2,7 9 9
×       5
```

Complete the chart.

Number	Expanded Form
	$2 + \frac{4}{10}$
	$2 + \frac{4}{100}$
3.6	
3.56	

Solve. Write your equations in the work space.

Molly's parents buy 4 concert tickets. The tickets cost $348 in all. How much does each ticket cost?

The bakery makes 535 cookies. The bakers pack 6 cookies in each box. How many boxes do they fill?

WORK SPACE

15.3

Lesson Activities

A

Eating breakfast

[ ] min.

Eating lunch

[ ] min.

Eating dinner

[ ] min.

Learning math

[ ] min.

7×6=?

Brushing teeth

[ ] sec.

Sleeping

[ ] hr.

B

How many minutes do you spend eating meals each day?

Do you spend more time eating or learning math each day?

How many hours and minutes do you spend eating meals each day?

How many minutes longer?

C

How many hours do you sleep in 1 week?

How many seconds do you spend brushing your teeth in 1 week?

How many days and hours do you sleep in 1 week?

How many minutes and seconds do you spend brushing your teeth in 1 week?

Practice 👤 Complete.

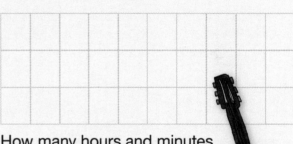

Solve. Write the equations you use.

Russell read a book for 45 min. on Friday, 1 hr. 20 min. on Saturday, and 1 hr. 5 min. on Sunday. How many hours and minutes did he read in all?

Elisha practices the guitar for 25 minutes each day. How many minutes does he practice in one week?

How many hours and minutes does he practice in one week?

⭐ It takes 13 hr. to drive to Jordyn's grandma's house. How many minutes does the drive take?

⭐ Each episode of Izzy's favorite show is 25 minutes long. How many seconds long is each episode?

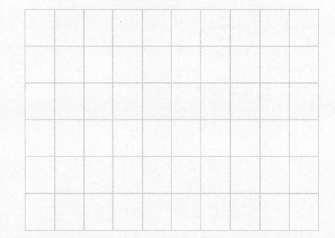

Review — Complete the equivalent fractions.

$$\frac{1}{2} = \frac{\boxed{}}{16}$$ $$\frac{1}{4} = \frac{\boxed{}}{16}$$ $$\frac{3}{4} = \frac{\boxed{}}{16}$$

$$\frac{1}{8} = \frac{\boxed{}}{16}$$ $$\frac{5}{8} = \frac{\boxed{}}{16}$$ $$\frac{8}{8} = \frac{\boxed{}}{16}$$

Follow the directions.

Draw a line that intersects $\overleftrightarrow{QR}$.	Draw a line that is parallel to $\overleftrightarrow{QR}$.	Draw a line that is perpendicular to $\overleftrightarrow{QR}$.
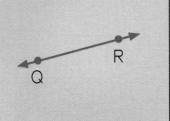	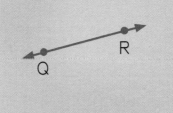	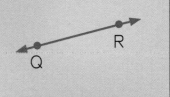

Complete.

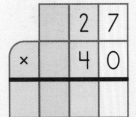 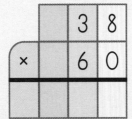 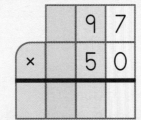

	2	7				3	8				9	7				8	1
×	4	0			×		6	0		×		5	0		×		6	0

Use the clues to answer the number riddles.

I am greater than 4 and less than 5.
I have two digits.
The digit in my tenths-place is 3 more than the digit in my ones-place.
What number am I?

I am greater than 50 and less than 70.
I am a multiple of 9.
I am even.
What number am I?

Lesson Activities

A

| kg = 1,000 g

| gram (g) | | kilogram (kg)

B

Type of Candy		Weight (kg and g)	Weight (g)
	Gummy bears	2 kg	
	Gummy fish	3 kg 175 g	
	Licorice		1,600 g
	Chocolate candies		2,500 g

C

A customer buys 1 kg 700 g of jelly beans and 1 kg 400 g of licorice.
What is the total weight of the candy?

		kg	700 g
+		kg	400 g
↻			

A customer buys 2 kg 200 g of chocolate candies. He eats 400 g.
What is the weight of the remaining candy?

	2 kg	200 g
−		400 g

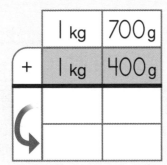

	2 kg	800 g
+		kg	900 g
↻		

	3 kg	
−		kg	100 g

Practice

Complete with <, >, or =.

999 g ◯ 1 kg | 1,000 g ◯ 1 kg | 1,001 g ◯ 1 kg

3,005 g ◯ 3 kg | 3,500 g ◯ 4 kg | 5,000 g ◯ 5 kg

Complete.

6 kg = ☐ g

6 kg 100 g = ☐ g

8 kg = ☐ g

8 kg 1 g = ☐ g

2,000 g = ☐ kg

2,455 g = ☐ kg ☐ g

9,000 g = ☐ kg

9,999 g = ☐ kg ☐ g

Complete.

	3 kg	500 g
+	4 kg	500 g
↻		

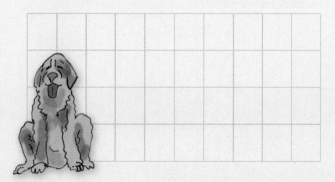

	7 kg	500 g
-	2 kg	250 g

	6 kg	
-	2 kg	700 g

Solve. Write the equations you use.

Edie's dog Max weighs 8 kg 400 g. Her dog Boots weighs 1 kg 600 g less than Max. How much does Boots weigh?

Finn's cat Mocha weighs 3 kg 950 g. His cat Pumpkin weighs 250 g more than Mocha. How much does Pumpkin weigh?

Review — Complete.

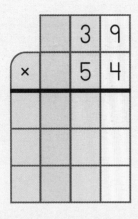

		3	9
×		5	4

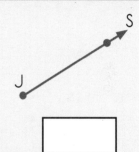

	70	8
20		
7		

78 × 27 = ☐

Label with letters and geometry symbols.

R

Z

☐

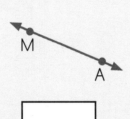

M

A

☐

S

J

☐

Use the printed rulers to measure the lines.

 in.

 __ in.

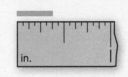 in.

 __ in.

 in.

 __ in.

Solve. Write the equations you use.

Nicholas uses $\frac{1}{3}$ lb. of clay for each pot he makes. How many pounds of clay does he need to make 10 pots?

The town is raising money for new playground equipment. The goal is $15,000. They have already raised $8,674. How much more money do they need to raise?

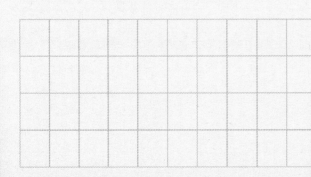

Lesson Activities

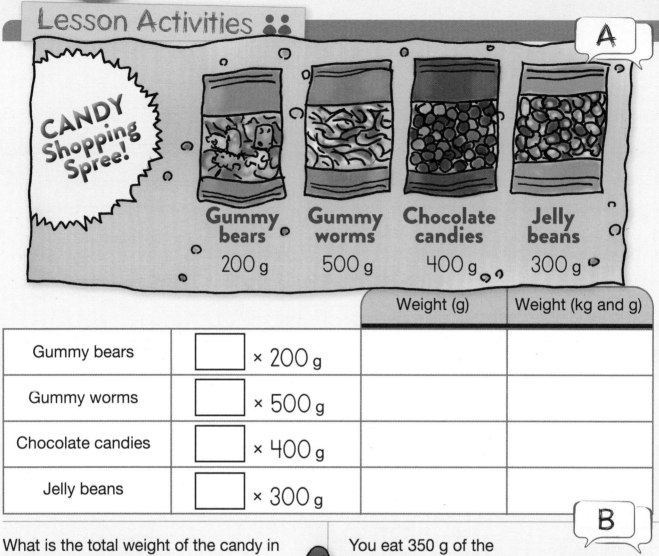

CANDY Shopping Spree!

Gummy bears 200 g Gummy worms 500 g Chocolate candies 400 g Jelly beans 300 g

		Weight (g)	Weight (kg and g)
Gummy bears	☐ × 200 g		
Gummy worms	☐ × 500 g		
Chocolate candies	☐ × 400 g		
Jelly beans	☐ × 300 g		

What is the total weight of the candy in kilograms and grams?

You eat 350 g of the gummy worms. What is the weight of the remaining gummy worms in grams?

You split the jelly beans equally with a friend. How many grams of jelly beans do you each get?

You divide the chocolate candies equally into 8 bags. How many grams of chocolate candies are in each bag?

Practice 👤 Use the grocery store ad to answer the questions.

Nuts and seeds on sale!

Almonds (2 kg)

Peanuts (1 kg 400 g)

Pistachios (700 g)

Pumpkin seeds (300 g)

Sunflower seeds (250 g)

Elliana buys 1 bag of peanuts. Her family eats 600 g. What is the weight of the remaining peanuts?

Avery buys 1 bag of almonds, 1 bag of peanuts, and 1 bag of pistachios. What is the total weight of the nuts in kilograms and grams?

Chandler buys 3 bags of pistachios. What is the total weight of the pistachios in kilograms and grams?

Odin buys 2 bags of sunflower seeds and 3 bags of pumpkin seeds. What is the total weight of the seeds in kilograms and grams?

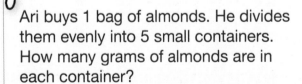

Fatimah buys 1 bag of peanuts. She divides them evenly into 2 bowls. How many grams of peanuts are in each bowl?

Ari buys 1 bag of almonds. He divides them evenly into 5 small containers. How many grams of almonds are in each container?

15.5

Label the numbers on the number line.

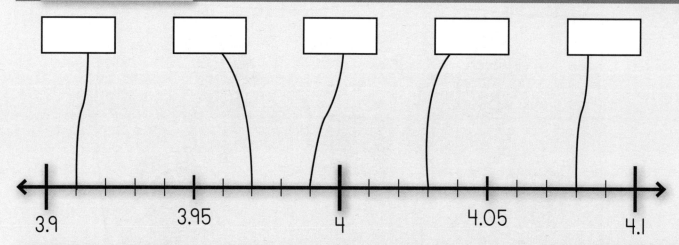

3.9   3.95   4   4.05   4.1

Use a protractor to measure the angles. Extend the sides as needed.

m∠ A = ⬜

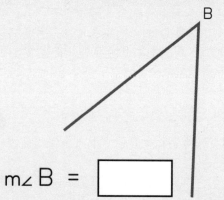

m∠ B = ⬜

Convert the mixed numbers to fractions.

$1\frac{1}{4}$ = ⬜ $2\frac{5}{6}$ = ⬜

$4\frac{1}{2}$ = ⬜ $5\frac{1}{10}$ = ⬜

Complete.

1 hr. 15 min. = ⬜ min.

2 hr. 50 min. = ⬜ min.

4 min. 30 sec. = ⬜ sec.

5 min. 6 sec. = ⬜ sec.

Lesson Activities 👥

1 liter (L)

1 milliliter (mL)

1 L = 1,000 mL

B

Drink	Capacity (L and mL)	Capacity (mL)
Lemon-lime soda	2 L	
Lemonade	1 L 550 mL	
Orange juice		1,750 mL
Pineapple juice		1,350 mL
Cranberry juice	1 L 50 mL	
Ginger ale		1,200 mL

CITRUS PUNCH RECIPE

★ 1 bottle lemon-lime soda
★ 1 container orange juice
★ 1 container lemonade

Makes:

[ ] L [ ] mL

C

Makes:

[ ] L [ ] mL

Practice   Complete.

$3 \text{ L} = \boxed{} \text{ mL}$

$3 \text{ L } 250 \text{ mL} = \boxed{} \text{ mL}$

$4{,}000 \text{ mL} = \boxed{} \text{ L}$

$4{,}500 \text{ mL} = \boxed{} \text{ L } \boxed{} \text{ mL}$

$9 \text{ L} = \boxed{} \text{ mL}$

$9 \text{ L } 990 \text{ mL} = \boxed{} \text{ mL}$

$8{,}000 \text{ mL} = \boxed{} \text{ L}$

$8{,}005 \text{ mL} = \boxed{} \text{ L } \boxed{} \text{ mL}$

Solve. Write the equations you use.

Mimi buys 1 L of apple juice and 850 mL of grape juice. How many milliliters of juice does she buy in all?

Zeke buys 1 L of grapefruit juice. He drinks 450 mL. How many milliliters of juice are left?

 Fatimah buys 2 liters of cola. She pours the cola into 8 cups, and she pours the same amount into each cup. How many milliliters are in each cup?

 William buys 6 cans of sparkling water. Each can holds 350 mL. How many milliliters of sparkling water does he buy?

How many liters and milliliters does he buy?

Review — Complete the equivalent fractions.

$\frac{2}{3} = \frac{\boxed{}}{6}$ $\frac{2}{3} = \frac{\boxed{}}{9}$ $\frac{2}{3} = \frac{\boxed{}}{12}$

$\frac{1}{4} = \frac{2}{\boxed{}}$ $\frac{1}{4} = \frac{5}{\boxed{}}$ $\frac{1}{4} = \frac{10}{\boxed{}}$

Connect each number to its dot on the number line.

| 0.2 | 0.49 | 0.77 | 0.55 | 0.98 |

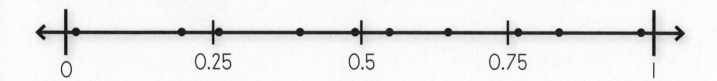

0   0.25   0.5   0.75   1

| 0.02 | 0.26 | 0.4 | 0.65 | 0.84 |

Draw the missing halves of these symmetric shapes.

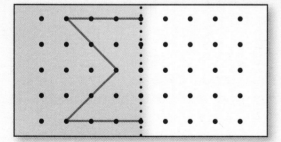

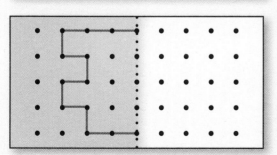

Complete.

$400 \div 2 = \boxed{}$

$450 \div 9 = \boxed{}$

$300 \div 6 = \boxed{}$

$2,500 \div 5 = \boxed{}$

$4,900 \div 7 = \boxed{}$

$4,000 \div 8 = \boxed{}$

Lesson Activities 👥

1 ounce (oz.)

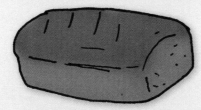

1 pound (lb.)

16 oz. = 1 lb.

Pounds	1	2	3	4	5	6
Ounces						

1 lb. 6 oz. = [   ] oz.

3 lb. 5 oz. = [   ] oz.

40 oz. = [   ] lb. [   ] oz.

92 oz. = [   ] lb. [   ] oz.

Keenan combines 7 balls of clay.
Each ball of clay weighs 5 ounces.
What is the total weight of the clay in ounces?

Caroline divides a 3-lb. block
of clay into 8 equal balls.
How many ounces does each ball weigh?

What is the total weight of the clay in
pounds and ounces?

Practice 👤 Complete the charts.

Pounds and Ounces	1 lb.	1 lb. 2 oz.	1 lb. 5 oz.	1 lb. 10 oz.	1 lb. 13 oz.
Ounces	16 oz.				

Pounds and Ounces	2 lb.				
Ounces	32 oz.	33 oz.	35 oz.	40 oz.	47 oz.

Solve. Write the equations you use.

Grant weighed 8 pounds 5 ounces when he was born. How many ounces did he weigh?

Jana's family buys a 25-lb. bag of rice. How many ounces of rice are in the bag?

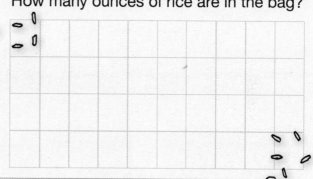

Amy's dad buys 10 lb. of strawberries to freeze. How many ounces of strawberries does he buy?

Jayson's mom buys 4 bags of spinach. Each bag weighs 6 ounces. How many ounces of spinach does she buy?

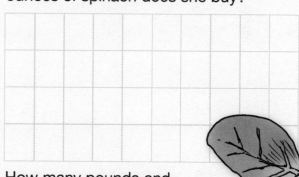

He splits the strawberries into 8 equal bags. How many ounces of strawberries are in each bag?

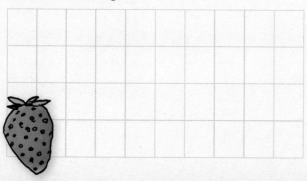

How many pounds and ounces of spinach does she buy?

15.7

Review

Write each length with a decimal point.

3 mm = ⬚ cm

8 mm = ⬚ cm

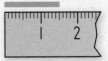

1 cm 5 mm = ⬚ cm

45 cm = ⬚ m

96 cm = ⬚ m

Use long division to solve.

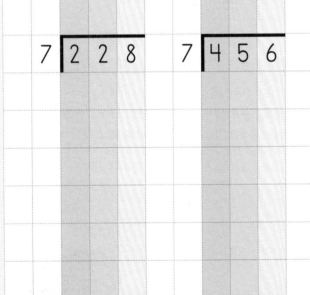

Round to the nearest whole number.

3.7 ≈ ⬚

12.96 ≈ ⬚

4.09 ≈ ⬚

8.34 ≈ ⬚

6.51 ≈ ⬚

10.5 ≈ ⬚

Write whether each triangle is acute, right, or obtuse.

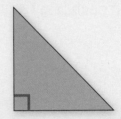

⬚ ⬚ ⬚

Lesson Activities

 1 cup (c.)   1 pint (pt.)    1 quart (qt.)    1 gallon (gal.)

1 pt.	= 2 c.
1 qt.	= 2 pt.
1 gal.	= 4 qt.

Pints	Cups		Quarts	Pints		Gallons	Quarts
1			1			1	
2			2			2	
3			3			3	
4			4			4	
5			5			5	

Race to 1 Gallon

 Player 1

 Player 2

Practice

Complete the charts. (The numbers are not in order.)

2 cups = 1 pint

Cups	6	10			
Pints			2	10	7

2 pints = 1 quart

Pints	8	14			
Quarts			3	6	8

4 quarts = 1 gallon

Quarts	8	20		
Gallons			3	5

Solve.

Dairy cows usually produce about
6 gallons of milk each day.
How many quarts do they produce?

Roger and his mom picked
25 quarts of blueberries.
How many pints did they pick?

Review   👤   **Complete.**

3	$\frac{2}{5}$
+ 1	$\frac{4}{5}$

6	$\frac{1}{8}$
+ 2	$\frac{4}{8}$

5	$\frac{3}{4}$
− 2	$\frac{1}{4}$

5	$\frac{1}{4}$
− 2	$\frac{3}{4}$

Write each decimal as a fraction or mixed number.

$0.7 = \dfrac{}{10}$

$0.63 = \boxed{}$

$1.74 = \boxed{}$

$0.32 = \boxed{}$

$0.5 = \boxed{}$

$3.29 = \boxed{}$

Solve. Write the equations you use.

The park is shaped like a square.
Its perimeter is 352 m.
What is the length of each side?

The skating rink is 27 ft. wide and
29 ft. long. What is its area?

29 ft.

27 ft.

Lesson Activities 👥

I fluid ounce (fl. oz.)   I cup (c.)

8 fl. oz. = I c.

Cups	1	2	3	4	5	6
Fluid Ounces						

Small
12 fl. oz.

☐ c.   ☐ fl. oz.

Medium
20 fl. oz.

☐ c.   ☐ fl. oz.

Large
24 fl. oz.

☐ c.   ☐ fl. oz.

Super-Large
44 fl. oz.

☐ c.   ☐ fl. oz.

Cam's mom drank 2 small coffees. How many cups of coffee did she drink?

How many cups larger is a super-large drink than a small drink?

Practice

Choose whether you would use ounces or fluid ounces for each measurement.

Capacity of a water bottle

| oz. | fl. oz. |

Weight of a bowl

| oz. | fl. oz. |

Weight of a vase

| oz. | fl. oz. |

Weight of a water bottle

| oz. | fl. oz. |

Capacity of a bowl

| oz. | fl. oz. |

Capacity of a vase

| oz. | fl. oz. |

Complete.

4 c. = ☐ fl. oz.

4 c. 1 fl. oz. = ☐ fl. oz.

9 c. = ☐ fl. oz.

9 c. 6 fl. oz. = ☐ fl. oz.

80 fl. oz. = ☐ c.

85 fl. oz. = ☐ c. ☐ fl. oz.

48 fl. oz. = ☐ c.

49 fl. oz. = ☐ c. ☐ fl. oz.

Solve. Write the equations you use.

Andrew has 5 c. of orange juice. He fills each glass with 6 fl. oz. How many glasses does he fill?

How many fluid ounces of orange juice does he have left?

There are 6 fl. oz. in each juice box. How many fluid ounces are in 10 juice boxes?

How many cups and fluid ounces are in 10 juice boxes?

Review

Use the numbers to complete the blanks. You will use each number only once.

| 2 | 5 | 6 | 32 | 300 | 3,000 |

3 L = [ ] mL   6,000 g = [ ] kg

48 hr. = [ ] days   5 min. = [ ] sec.

2 lb. = [ ] oz.   40 fl. oz. = [ ] c.

**Use the words in the word bank to label each shape.
Use the most specific name possible for each shape.**

| rhombus | parallelogram | quadrilateral |

      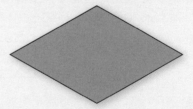

[ ]   [ ]   [ ]

Complete the circles with <, >, or =.

$\frac{1}{2}$ ◯ 0.7 $\frac{1}{2}$ ◯ 0.4 $\frac{1}{2}$ ◯ 0.39

$\frac{1}{2}$ ◯ 0.99 $\frac{1}{2}$ ◯ 0.50 $\frac{1}{2}$ ◯ 0.05

Unit Wrap-Up

Write each unit in the correct part of the chart.

Units of Time	Units of Weight	Units of Capacity

hr.   c.   sec.   day   pt.

L   oz.   mL   qt.   min.

lb.   gal.   kg   fl. oz.   g

Complete.

1 hr. = ☐ min.

4 hr. = ☐ min.

☐ hr. = 180 min.

1 c. = ☐ fl. oz.

5 c. = ☐ fl.oz.

☐ c. = 32 fl. oz.

1 L = ☐ mL

9 L = ☐ mL

☐ L = 4,000 mL

1 kg = ☐ g

8 kg = ☐ g

☐ kg = 7,000 g

1 lb. = ☐ oz.

2 lb. = ☐ oz.

☐ lb. = 160 oz.

1 min. = ☐ sec.

2 min. = ☐ sec.

☐ min. = 600 sec.

Unit Wrap-Up

Solve. Write the equations you use.

YOU'RE INVITED TO WYATT'S WATER FUN BIRTHDAY PARTY!

We'll have water balloons, relay races, and sprinkler games.

Make sure to wear a swimsuit and bring a towel!

Wyatt's parents buy 6 bottles of lemonade for the party. Each bottle holds 500 mL of lemonade. How many liters of lemonade do they buy?

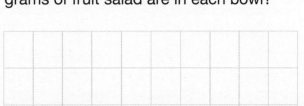

Wyatt's parents make 2 kg 400 g of fruit salad for the party. They split the fruit salad equally into 4 bowls. How many grams of fruit salad are in each bowl?

The blue team takes 3 min. 10 sec. to finish the relay race. The purple team takes 2 min. 45 sec. How much longer does the blue team take than the purple team?

★ The total weight of the water balloons is 35 lb. What is the total weight of the water balloons in ounces?

★ Each water balloon weighs 5 oz. How many water balloons are there?

Lesson Activities 👥

Maya - 0   Seth - 2
Josh - 0   Thea - 3
Erin - 0   Uma - 3
Mae - 0   Hope - 4
Lila - 1   Eli - 4
SJ - 1   Bob - 6

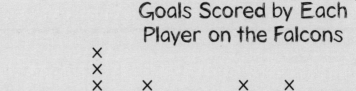

Goals Scored by Each Player on the Falcons

Number of Goals

What's the greatest number of goals scored by a player?

How many players scored fewer than 3 goals?

How many players are on the team?

What's the fewest number of goals scored by a player?

How many players scored 3 or more goals?

How many goals did the team score in all?

Jay - 4   Amie - 6

Abi - 2   Chris - 3

Levi - 5   Eva - 1

Wren - 5   Toba - 0

Cory - 2   Gaia - 2

Goals Scored by Each Player on the Eagles

Number of Goals

What's the greatest number of goals scored by a player?

How many players scored fewer than 3 goals?

How many players are on the team?

What's the fewest number of goals scored by a player?

How many players scored 3 or more goals?

How many goals did the team score in all?

Practice 👤

Lydia went fishing with her grandpa.
She made a line plot to show the lengths of the fish.
Use the line plot to answer the questions.

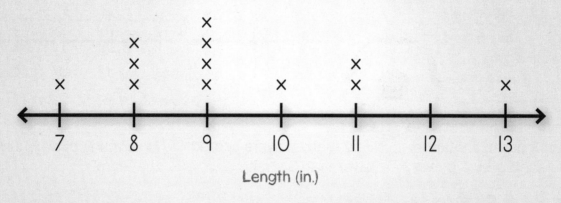

Lengths of the Fish We Caught

Length (in.)

How many fish were 8 inches long?	How many fish were 12 inches long?
How many fish were longer than 9 inches?	How many fish were shorter than 9 inches?
How many inches long was the shortest fish?	How many inches long was the longest fish?
How much longer was the longest fish than the shortest fish?	How many fish did they catch in all?

Review 👤 Complete.

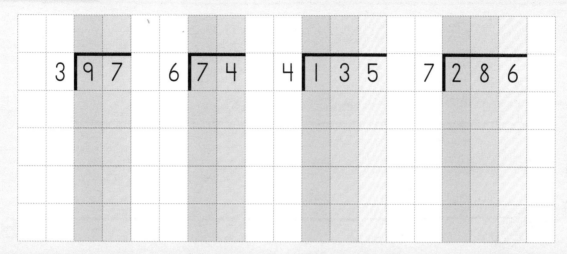

| | 3 | 9 | 7 | | 6 | 7 | 4 | | 4 | 1 | 3 | 5 | | 7 | 2 | 8 | 6 |

Complete.

I cm = [ ] mm

I m = [ ] cm

I km = [ ] m

I kg = [ ] g

I L = [ ] mL

4 cm 7 mm = [ ] mm

2 L 50 mL = [ ] mL

3 m 19 cm = [ ] cm

2,500 g = [ ] kg [ ] g

730 m = [ ] km [ ] m

1,730 m = [ ] km [ ] m

Solve. Write the equations you use.

Toni runs 8 laps. Each lap is 400 m long. How many kilometers and meters does she run?

Griffin buys 3 kg of rice. He divides the rice equally into 6 bags. How many grams of rice are in each bag?

Lesson Activities

A

Height of Bean Plants in the Sun

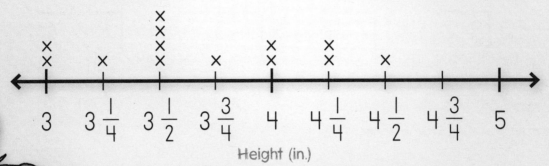

Height (in.)

B

Height of Bean Plants in the Dark

Height (in.)

Data

$4\frac{1}{2}$	4	$3\frac{1}{4}$	5	$3\frac{3}{4}$	5	$4\frac{1}{4}$	$4\frac{3}{4}$
$4\frac{3}{4}$	4	$4\frac{1}{2}$	$4\frac{3}{4}$	$4\frac{1}{2}$	4	$3\frac{3}{4}$	$4\frac{1}{2}$

C

Plants in the Sun

Height of tallest plant	
Height of shortest plant	
Number of plants shorter than 4 in.	
Number of plants at least 4 in. tall	
Total number of plants	

Plants in the Dark

Height of tallest plant	
Height of shortest plant	
Number of plants shorter than 4 in.	
Number of plants at least 4 in. tall	
Total number of plants	

Practice A scientist measured grasshoppers' lengths for a research study. Use his data to make a line plot. Then, use the line plot to answer the questions.

Grasshopper Lengths

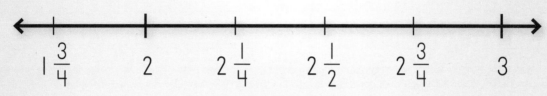

Length (cm)

Data								
2	$2\frac{1}{4}$	$2\frac{3}{4}$	$2\frac{1}{2}$	3	2	$1\frac{3}{4}$	$2\frac{1}{4}$
$2\frac{1}{4}$	$2\frac{1}{2}$	2	3	$2\frac{1}{4}$	$2\frac{1}{4}$	2	

How many grasshoppers were exactly $2\frac{3}{4}$ centimeters long?

How many grasshoppers were exactly 2 centimeters long?

How many grasshoppers were shorter than 2 centimeters?

How many grasshoppers were longer than 2 centimeters?

How many centimeters long was the shortest grasshopper?

How many centimeters long were the longest grasshoppers?

How much longer was the longest grasshopper than the shortest grasshopper?

How many grasshoppers did the scientist measure?

Review 👤 Solve.

```
    4 5          5 6          7 1          8 4
×     9 1    ×     6 0    ×     2 2    ×     8 4
```

Complete.

| 1 ft. = [____] in. |
| 1 yd. = [____] ft. |
| 1 yd. = [____] in. |
| 1 mi. = [____] ft. |
| 1 lb. = [____] oz. |
| 1 c. = [____] fl. oz. |

2 c. 3 fl. oz. = [____] fl. oz.

3 ft. 2 in. = [____] in.

1 mi. 100 ft. = [____] ft.

43 in. = [____] yd. [____] in.

20 oz. = [____] lb. [____] oz.

24 ft. = [____] yd.

Solve. Write the equations you use.

David runs 20 sprints.
Each sprint is 50 yards long.
How many feet does David run?

Ruby buys 2 lb. of coffee.
She divides the coffee equally into 8 bags.
How many ounces of coffee are in each bag?

Lesson Activities 👥

Goals Scored by Each Player on the Falcons

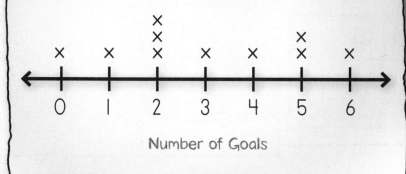

Number of Goals

Total number of goals	24
Number of players	12
Average number of goals per player	

Goals Scored by Each Player on the Eagles

Number of Goals

Total number of goals	30
Number of players	10
Average number of goals per player	

How Many Children Are In Your Family?

2	1	6
3	3	4
2	3	3
4	2	

Total number of children	
Number of families	
Average number of children per family	

Practice 👤

Zachary's family keeps chickens.
He records how many eggs the chickens produce each day.
Use his data to complete the blanks.

Week 1

M	T	W	Th	F	Sa	Su
7	8	9	7	10	6	9

Total number of eggs	
Number of days	
Average number of eggs per day	

Week 2

M	T	W	Th	F	Sa	Su
10	8	9	10	7	9	10

Total number of eggs	
Number of days	
Average number of eggs per day	

Week 3

M	T	W	Th	F	Sa	Su
8	5	10	7	6	6	7

Total number of eggs	
Number of days	
Average number of eggs per day	

Review · Complete the equivalent fractions.

$\frac{1}{4} = \frac{\boxed{}}{20}$ $\frac{1}{4} = \frac{\boxed{}}{40}$ $\frac{1}{4} = \frac{\boxed{}}{24}$

$\frac{3}{4} = \frac{\boxed{}}{20}$ $\frac{3}{4} = \frac{\boxed{}}{40}$ $\frac{3}{4} = \frac{\boxed{}}{24}$

Write the numbers in order from least to greatest.

0.74 0.07

0.7 0.4

☐ ☐ ☐ ☐
least   greatest

1.26 1.8

1.09 1.90

☐ ☐ ☐ ☐
least   greatest

Solve. Write your equations in the work space.

A baker makes 149 muffins. She puts 6 muffins in each box.

- How many boxes does she fill?

- How many muffins are left over?

She makes 186 cookies. She arranges all the cookies on 8 trays, as equally as possible. How many cookies are on each tray?

WORK SPACE

Lesson Activities 👥

Bowling Scores

Monday: 94, 67, 103

Average: [ ]

Wednesday: 79, 84, 92

Average: [ ]

Thursday: 85, 99

Average: [ ]

Saturday: 71, 110, 95, 104

Average: [ ]

WORK SPACE

SPIN TO WIN!

60, 25, 80, 45, 50, 15, 75, 20

Player 1

Sum: [ ]   Average: [ ]

Player 2

Sum: [ ]   Average: [ ]

Practice 👤 Use the data to answer the questions. You may use mental math or write your equations in the workspace.

Clark kept track of how many points he scored in each basketball game.

Game 1: 6 pts. Game 4: 12 pts.

Game 2: 10 pts. Game 5: 3 pts.

Game 3: 8 pts. Game 6: 9 pts.

How many points did he score in all?

On average, how many points did he score in each game?

Georgia recorded how many hours she read each week.

Week 1 – 6 hr. Week 3 – 5 hr.

Week 2 – 8 hr. Week 4 – 9 hr.

How many hours did she read in all?

On average, how many hours did she read each week?

Ved held a lemonade stand for 5 days. He wrote down how much money he earned each day.

Day 1 – $23   Day 4 – $28

Day 2 – $37   Day 5 – $32

Day 3 – $15

How much money did he earn in all?

On average, how much money did he earn each day?

WORK SPACE

Review

Complete. Convert your answer to a mixed number or whole number if possible.

$3 \times \dfrac{2}{3} =$ ☐ = ☐ $6 \times \dfrac{2}{3} =$ ☐ = ☐

$9 \times \dfrac{2}{3} =$ ☐ = ☐ $12 \times \dfrac{2}{3} =$ ☐ = ☐

Complete.

	3 L	800 mL
+	4 L	200 mL
↻		

	3 kg	500 g
–	1 kg	250 g

	5 km	200 m
–	2 km	700 m

Complete.

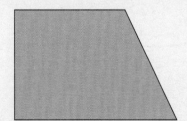

☐ pair(s) of parallel sides

☐ right angle(s)

☐ pair(s) of parallel sides

☐ right angle(s)

☐ pair(s) of parallel sides

☐ right angle(s)

Unit Wrap-Up

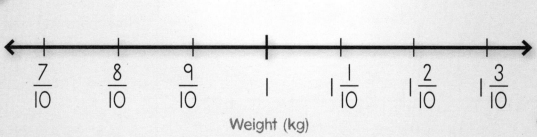

The grocer weighed the bags of grapes at her store. Use the data to make a line plot. Then, answer the questions.

Weight of Bags of Grapes

$$\frac{7}{10} \quad \frac{8}{10} \quad \frac{9}{10} \quad 1 \quad 1\frac{1}{10} \quad 1\frac{2}{10} \quad 1\frac{3}{10}$$

Weight (kg)

Data

$\frac{9}{10}$	1	$\frac{7}{10}$	$1\frac{2}{10}$	1	$1\frac{1}{10}$
$1\frac{2}{10}$	$1\frac{3}{10}$	$1\frac{1}{10}$	$\frac{9}{10}$	$1\frac{2}{10}$	$\frac{9}{10}$

How many bags weigh more than 1 kg?

How many bags weigh less than 1 kg?

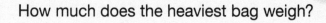

How much does the heaviest bag weigh?

How much does the lightest bag weigh?

How much heavier is the heaviest bag than the lightest bag?

How many bags did the grocer weigh?

Unit Wrap-Up

Use the line plot to answer the questions.

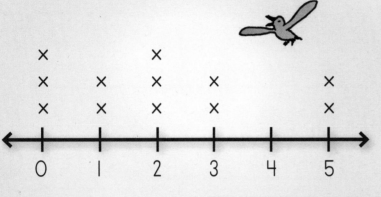

Number of Pets in Each Family

```
 ×           ×
 ×     ×     ×     ×           ×
 ×     ×     ×     ×           ×
←——+———+———+———+———+———+——→
   0   1   2   3   4   5
```

Number of Pets

What is the total number of pets in all the families?

How many families are there?

What is the average number of pets per family?

Use the data to answer the questions. Write your equations in the work space.

Lillian's lacrosse team played 5 games. Their scores were 9, 12, 15, 7, and 12 points. What was the team's average score?

WORK SPACE

Ben's volleyball team played 4 matches. Their scores were 20, 25, 14, and 25. What was the team's average score?

Lesson Activities

Leaf Fight

Practice   Match.

20 × 30	500	4,000 ÷ 5
400 × 5	600	8,000 ÷ 4
50 × 10	800	2,400 ÷ 4
30 × 50	1,500	3,000 ÷ 6
40 × 20	2,000	9,000 ÷ 3
500 × 6	2,400	3,000 ÷ 2
60 × 40	3,000	4,800 ÷ 2

Find the missing digits or numbers.

★

	7
	350
5	350

☐ × ☐ = 4,235

★

×		3	☐
		2	7
+	8	1	0
	8	3	7

(with ☐ 7 on top)

★

		1	☐
4	☐	8
−	4	
	3	8
−	3	6
		☐

Review 👤 — Circle the numbers that match the description. X the numbers that do not match the description.

Multiple of 8			Factors of 20			Divisible by 5		
2	4	16	4	5	10	30	35	54
40	48	80	30	40	80	90	200	300

Complete.

All sides are equal.

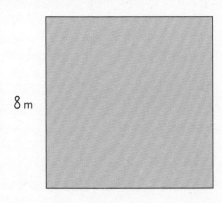

8 m

Perimeter: _____

Area: _____

12 ft.

8 ft.

5 ft.

3 ft.
3 ft.

9 ft.

Perimeter: _____

Area: _____

Use the clues to complete the chart.

- Mom is 4 times as old as Siena.
- Siena is twice as old as Ollie.
- Grandpa is 12 times as old as Ollie.
- Dad is 23 years younger than Grandpa.

Name	Age
Ollie	
Siena	
Mom	40
Dad	
Grandpa	

Lesson Activities

$1\frac{7}{8}$ = ☐

$2\frac{3}{5}$ = ☐

$\frac{9}{3}$ = ☐

$\frac{13}{4}$ = ☐

$\frac{3}{4}$ = $\frac{\ }{8}$

$\frac{1}{3}$ = $\frac{5}{\ }$

$\frac{5}{6}$ = $\frac{\ }{12}$

$\frac{4}{5}$ = $\frac{20}{\ }$

0.7 = ☐

0.07 = ☐

1.49 = ☐

2.03 = ☐

Fraction and Decimal Four in a Row

$\frac{13}{4}$	1.49	$\frac{3}{4}$	$\frac{9}{3}$	$\frac{7}{10}$	$2\frac{3}{5}$
3	$1\frac{7}{8}$	2.03	$\frac{5}{15}$	0.07	$\frac{10}{12}$
$\frac{5}{6}$	$\frac{6}{8}$	0.7	$1\frac{49}{100}$	$\frac{15}{8}$	$\frac{4}{5}$
$\frac{13}{5}$	$\frac{7}{100}$	$2\frac{3}{100}$	$\frac{20}{25}$	$\frac{1}{3}$	$3\frac{1}{4}$

Practice 👤   Complete.

	1	$\frac{3}{4}$
+	2	$\frac{1}{4}$
↻		

	3	$\frac{1}{8}$
+	3	$\frac{4}{8}$
↻		

	6	$\frac{2}{5}$
−	3	$\frac{1}{5}$

	4	$\frac{1}{10}$
−	2	$\frac{7}{10}$

Solve. Use common denominators.

Trail	Length
Glacier Trail	$\frac{5}{12}$ mi.
Alpine Trail	$\frac{3}{4}$ mi.
Ridge Trail	$\frac{2}{3}$ mi.

$\frac{5}{12}$ ⬇ ☐ $\frac{3}{4}$ ⬇ ☐ $\frac{2}{3}$ ⬇ ☐

Which trail is shortest?

Which trail is longest?

Solve. Write the equations you use.

Rose buys 15 bags of almonds.
Each bag weighs $\frac{1}{3}$ lb.
How many pounds of almonds
does she buy?

Reese has $3\frac{1}{8}$ qt. of juice.
He uses $1\frac{7}{8}$ qt. to make punch.
How many quarts of juice are left?

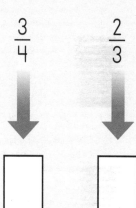

Review

Color the decimal squares to match.
Then, write a fraction or mixed number to match.

0.01 = ☐

0.87 = ☐

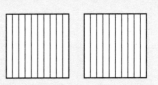

1.2 = ☐

Connect each number to its dot on the number line.

0.5	0.95	0.84	1.06

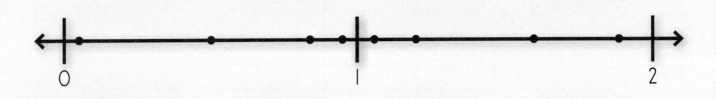

0   1   2

0.05	1.2	1.6	1.89

Use the clues to answer the number riddles.

I am greater than 1 and less than 2.
I have 2 digits.
The digit in my tenths-place is 4 times
the digit in my ones-place.
What number am I?

I am greater than 2 and less than 3.
I have 3 digits.
One of my digits is a zero.
One of my digits is a 6.
I am less than $2\frac{1}{2}$.
What number am I?

Lesson Activities 👥

Measurement Tag

Centimeters

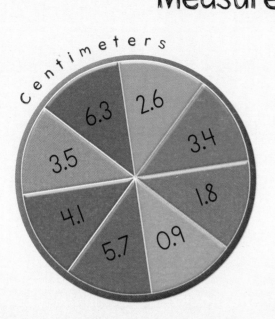

Inches

PLAYER
2
START

PLAYER
1
START

B

What was your favorite math activity this year?

What math topic was most interesting to you this year?

What math skill did you work hardest to learn this year?

What do you hope to learn in math next year?

 Practice : Complete. Then, write the problem's letter in the blanks that match your answer.

E 4 min. = [   ] sec.

G 48 hr. = [   ] days

V 5,000 g = [   ] kg

T 10 lb. = [   ] oz.

H 5 c. = [   ] fl. oz.

S 3,000 mL = [   ] L

I 3 ft. 2 in. = [   ] in.

N 4 m 3 cm = [   ] cm

¤ Why is six afraid of seven?

¤ Because...

[ ][ ][ ][ ][ ]   [ ][ ][ ][ ][ ]   [ ][ ][ ][ ]
3 240 5 240 403   240 38 2 40 160   403 38 403 240

CONGRATULATIONS!

Presented to

_____

for successfully completing

Fourth Grade Math
with Confidence

_____   _____

Date   Signature